Anxious Attachment Recovery

A Practical Guide to Emotional Freedom and
Lasting Relationships

Amy Harper

Contents

Exclusive Offer

Thank you for purchasing this book!

As complementary content for the book you are about to read, I'd like to offer you the following, which you can download directly to your mailbox. Communication is essential to improve your relationships and overcome your anxious attachment style. Please follow the instructions below for instant access to the Ebook + Audiobook.

2 in 1 Package
Ebook +
Audiobook

Are you ready to take decisive steps to improve the communication on your relationship?

Get **FREE** copies of Communication Skills for Lasting Love in two formats: ebook and audiobook. So you can read at the comfort of your home or listen to it on the go.

Learn tools and techniques that you can start implementing **TODAY**.

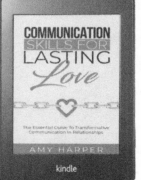

Discover how to:
- enhance your active listening skills.
- set boundaries effectively.
- positively impact your relationships.

Scan below to get access:

Join hundreds of others in this self-improvement journey!

Introduction

"As we familiarize ourselves more with secure attachment, our relationships become easier and more rewarding—we're less reactive, more receptive, more available for connection, healthier, and much more likely to bring out the securely attached tendencies in others."
Diane Poole Heller.

Understanding and awareness of anxious attachment can aid individuals in building healthier and more secure relationships. This book will provide comprehensive insights into anxious attachment, helping individuals overcome it and establish lasting and fulfilling relationships.

While characterized by sensitivity and attentiveness to their partner's needs, an anxious attachment style often necessitates constant reassurance and affection to feel secure within a romantic relationship. Failure to receive validation in the desired manner can cause feelings of worry and stress for those with an anxious attachment style.

Individuals with an anxious attachment style often internalize a perceived lack of affection and intimacy as a sign that they are unworthy of love, leading to intense fears of rejection. To avoid abandonment, they may exhibit clinginess, hypervigilance, and jealousy within their relationships. The anxiety of being alone drives attachers to exert significant efforts to maintain their relationships, viewing their partner as the solution to their emotional needs. I'll touch upon these efforts throughout the book.

Anxious Attachment in Relationships

Although individuals with an anxious attachment style yearn for romantic connections, they often find relationships to be a source of stress and anxiety.

Anxious attachers possess a high level of sensitivity and attentiveness to their partner's needs, willingly accommodating them. However, their insecurities and doubts about their self-worth lead them to project these uncertainties onto their partner's behavior. If their partner fails to respond to their needs in the specific way they desire, it reinforces their belief that they are unworthy of love.

For individuals with an anxious attachment style, relationships are a double-edged sword. On one hand, they deeply fear rejection and abandonment, leading to hypervigilance and a constant need for reassurance from their partner. They constantly seek validation and confirmation of their partner's love. On the other hand, being in the presence of their loved one provides solace and comfort. The presence of their partner serves as a balm to their anxieties.

Who Is This Book For?

This book is for anyone feeling stuck in a cycle of worry and uncertainty in their relationships, especially if you often feel insecure or anxious about your partner's feelings for you. If you've ever felt like you're constantly waiting for reassurance or overthinking things in your relationships, this guide can help. It's also great if you've faced challenges trusting others or want to understand why you feel like you do in relationships. Think of it as a roadmap to understanding yourself better and building healthier connections with others.

Why Do You Need This Book?

Your feelings of insecurity or anxiety in relationships can stem from patterns developed over time, possibly from past experiences or early relationships. This book offers practical insights and tools to help you recognize and understand these patterns better. By gaining this understanding, you can start making positive changes in how you approach relationships, helping you feel more secure, confident, and fulfilled in your connections with others. It's a step-by-step guide to addressing those underlying concerns and building healthier relationship habits.

What's Next?

Let us delve into the book's first chapter, where we will explore all aspects of anxious attachment and equip ourselves with the tools to overcome its challenges and foster healthier relationships.

Chapter 1

What is Anxious Attachment?

"The key to finding a mate who can fulfill those needs is to first fully acknowledge your need for intimacy, availability, and security in a relationship - and to believe that they are legitimate. They aren't good or bad, they are simply your needs. Don't let people make you feel guilty for acting "needy" or dependent." Don't be ashamed of feeling incomplete when you're not in a relationship, or for wanting to be close to your partner and to depend on him."

Amir Levine & Rachel S.F. Heller.

Anxious attachment refers to a specific type of insecure relationship children develop with their mothers or primary caregivers. This attachment style can have significant and lasting effects on their relationships as adults. Attachment is the innate ability to form emotional bonds with others, and it begins at birth and continues to shape how individuals relate to others throughout their lives. I will speak about relationships and how insecurity develops later in the book.

The attachment style that is established in early childhood, particularly with the primary caregiver, serves as a blueprint for future relationships. If the emotional needs of the child are consistently not met or responded to, it can lead to the development of an insecure attachment style, specifically anxious attachment.

Individuals with anxious attachment may struggle with trust, intimacy, and forming secure emotional connections in their adult relationships. They may constantly fear abandonment or rejection and feel the need for reassurance and constant attention to alleviate their anxieties. This can create challenges in establishing and maintaining healthy, fulfilling relationships.

It is important to note that while anxious attachment can have its challenges, it is not a life sentence. With self-awareness and a willingness to heal and grow, individuals with an anxious attachment can work towards developing more secure attachment patterns. This may involve seeking therapy or counseling, learning effective communication and emotional regulation skills, and building relationships with securely attached individuals who can serve as positive role models.

Attachment Styles

Attachment styles can significantly impact how individuals behave and react to relationships, particularly in romantic contexts. There are four main attachment styles: Secure, Anxious, Avoidant, and Disorganized (Cherry, 2022). Understanding these patterns can help individuals identify their needs and overcome relationship challenges.

Secure attachment is characterized by individuals with high self-worth and can set boundaries. They feel satisfied in their close relationships and have a sense of safety and stability. Usually, as children, their caregivers were consistent and healthily responded to their needs.

Anxious attachment is characterized by neediness, anxiety, and low self-esteem. Individuals with this attachment style want to be close to others but fear rejection. As children, their caregivers were likely inconsistent in their responses, leading to feelings of anxiety and uncertainty.

Avoidant attachment is characterized by individuals who avoid emotional closeness with others. They might rely on themselves, crave freedom, and struggle with emotions. In childhood, their caregivers were likely unavailable, rejecting their needs and emotions, leading to a learned avoidance of closeness.

Disorganized attachment is characterized by an intense fear of being unloved, often stemming from childhood trauma, abuse, or neglect. Individuals with this attachment style might feel they don't deserve love. They likely had caregivers with chaotic or scary behavior, leading to emotional problems in adulthood.

By understanding their attachment style, individuals can identify their needs and behaviors in relationships and work towards healthier patterns. Seeking therapy or counseling can also help develop more secure attachment styles and build fulfilling relationships.

Impact of Anxious Attachment

An anxious attachment can significantly impact a person's ability to handle stress and adapt to change. This can manifest in difficulties in various relationships, including romantic relationships, friendships, and other connections.

Anxious or disorganized attachments often arise as a result of certain factors, such as trauma, neglect, early separation from parents, lengthy hospitalizations, inconsistent or inexperienced parenting, emotional unavailability from caregivers, or a caregiver's depression (Brennan, 2021).

If a person faced challenges or struggles during their early childhood, as an adult, they might find it difficult to trust others. Some signs of an anxious attachment include a fear of emotions, intimacy, and emotional closeness, a desire to distance oneself when someone becomes needy, a sense of independence and not relying on others, disregarding other people's feelings, having weak boundaries, requiring constant reassurance, being needy or clingy, becoming fixated or overly obsessed with someone, craving intimacy but struggling to trust others, and experiencing anxiety or jealousy when away from their partner. The signs may vary in different individuals (*Do Your Early Experiences Affect Your Adult Relationships?*, 2016).

It's important to note that having an anxious attachment does not necessarily indicate a lack of love during childhood. Instead, it suggests that the person did not receive all the emotional support and responsiveness they needed. Additionally, personality and other life experiences may contribute to developing anxious attachment.

Preventing Anxious Attachment From Affecting Relationships

If you have an anxious attachment style, there are specific steps you can take to navigate your relationships.

To start, learning effective communication skills can be tremendously helpful. Learning to express your emotions and ask for what you need can help you become more transparent and clear in your relationships. Additionally, understanding nonverbal cues, such as posture and gestures, can enable you to read your partner's feelings more accurately and respond sensibly. You should also be aware of your body language and how it communicates with your partner.

Another effective way to deal with an anxious attachment style is to see a therapist. A therapist can help you understand and process early childhood experiences that may have contributed to this attachment style, allowing you to recognize and resolve these negative patterns.

It may also be helpful to seek out a secure attachment in your relationships. This can be done with some guidance. While it may be uncomfortable at first, engaging in a relationship with someone who is securely attached can provide a sense of what a stable and healthy relationship feels like. Additionally, building friendships with individuals with high self-esteem, healthy boundaries, and secure attachment styles can be beneficial in shifting your attachment patterns towards a more positive direction.

Self-Assessment Tool

Here's a self-assessment tool to help you determine your anxious attachment style. Remember, this shouldn't be used as a professional diagnosis. So, let's dive in!

1)How do you typically react when someone you're dating takes longer than usual to respond to a text or call?

a) No big deal, I'm patient and understanding.

b) I worry and overanalyze their behavior, wondering if they're losing interest.

c) I feel anxious and insecure, thinking they're intentionally trying to ignore me.

2) How would you describe your approach to relationships?

a) I feel comfortable and confident expressing my needs while respecting my partner's boundaries.

b) I tend to seek reassurance from my partner and worry about their level of commitment.

c) I often feel clingy and find trusting my partner's love and affection challenging.

3) In a romantic relationship, do you often seek validation or reassurance from your partner?

a) Rarely, if ever. I'm pretty independent and secure.

b) Occasionally, especially when I'm feeling unsure or insecure.

c) Frequently, it's almost a daily necessity for me.

4) How do you usually feel when your partner spends time with friends or family without you?

a) I enjoy my alone time and trust that they value our relationship.

b) I feel uneasy but understand the importance of maintaining separate social lives.

c) I often feel anxious and worry that they might prefer the company of others over me.

5) How do you typically handle disagreements or conflicts in a relationship?

a) I communicate openly and calmly, aiming for resolution and understanding.

b) I tend to overthink and worry that any disagreement could lead to a bigger problem.

c) I feel overwhelmed and often fear that a conflict will end the relationship.

6) How do you usually feel when you are unable to spend time with your partner?

a) It's disappointing, but I understand we both have our own lives to attend to.

b) I start to miss them and may occasionally worry about the distance affecting our connection.

c) I feel incredibly anxious and fear that they might forget about me or find someone else.

Results:

Mostly A's: You lean towards a secure attachment style. You value independence and trust in your relationships while maintaining healthy emotional connections.

Mostly B's: You lean towards having an anxious attachment style. You may occasionally experience worry or insecurity in relationships, but you can overcome these challenges with awareness and communication.

Mostly C's: It seems like you have an anxious attachment. You may often feel anxious, doubt your partner's love, and seek constant reassurance. It could be helpful to work on building self-confidence and addressing underlying anxieties to establish healthier relationship patterns.

Remember, this assessment is just a tool to give you some insights into your attachment style.

Signs in Children

Various signs may indicate a child has an attachment disorder. These signs include engaging in bullying or aggressive behavior towards others, displaying extreme clinginess and attachment to caregivers, failing to smile or show positive emotions, experiencing intense outbursts of anger, avoiding eye contact, showing no fear of strangers, lacking affection towards primary caregivers, exhibiting oppositional behaviors, struggling with impulse control, engaging in self-destructive behaviors, observing others playing but choosing not to join in, and displaying withdrawn or listless moods.

It is important to note that attachment disorders that develop during childhood can persist and impact a person's relationships in adulthood.

However, it should be emphasized that the specific attachment styles experienced in childhood do not always directly translate to attachment patterns in adulthood. This means that individuals with different childhood attachment experiences can still develop a variety of attachment styles in their adult relationships.

Signs in Adults

Adults with attachment issues may exhibit a range of signs and challenges related to forming and maintaining emotional bonds with others. One common manifestation is difficulty in establishing healthy boundaries. This can manifest as having weak boundaries, leading to problems asserting one's needs and maintaining personal space, or having rigid and overly strict boundaries that can hinder closeness and intimacy with others.

Additionally, adults with attachment issues may engage in risky behaviors as a way to cope with their difficulties in forming and maintaining relationships. These behaviors can include impulsivity, seeking out unhealthy or toxic relationships, or engaging in self-destructive behaviors as a means of seeking emotional connection or relief from attachment-related struggles.

Research surrounding attachment issues in adulthood is ongoing, but evidence suggests that individuals with attachment issues may face challenges in forming and maintaining romantic relationships (*Attachment Disorder in Adults: Symptoms, Causes, and More*, 2020). These individuals may struggle with trust, finding it difficult to rely on and have confidence in their partners entirely. They may also experience heightened levels of anxiety within their relationships, often feeling insecure or fearful of rejection or abandonment.

Seeking constant reassurance from their partners or engaging in behaviors to distance themselves emotionally can be common as they try to protect themselves from becoming too attached or getting hurt.

It's important to note that while these signs and challenges are commonly associated with attachment issues in adults, individual experiences and circumstances can vary.

Causes

Attachment issues can arise from various factors, but childhood experiences primarily influence them. One main factor is the presence of inconsistent or neglectful caregivers. This means that when children have caregivers who are unreliable or fail to meet their emotional and physical needs consistently, they are more likely to develop attachment disorders. These disorders can then continue into adulthood if not addressed.

It is worth noting that not all children who experience inconsistent or neglectful caregiving develop attachment disorders. However, researchers have found a clear link between attachment disorders and certain adverse experiences (Erozkan, 2016). For example, significant neglect or deprivation, frequent changes in primary caregivers, or being raised in institutional settings can all contribute to the development of attachment disorders.

Aside from these experiences, other factors may increase the risk of developing attachment disorders. One such factor is experiencing abuse, whether physical, emotional, or sexual. Children who are subjected to abuse are at a higher risk of developing attachment issues (Riggs, 2010).

Additionally, caregivers who lack proper parenting skills, struggle with anger management, or display neglectful behavior are also more likely to contribute to the development of attachment issues. Furthermore, parents who have psychiatric conditions may find it challenging to provide consistent and secure attachment experiences for their children.

Another potential risk factor that has been identified is prenatal exposure to alcohol or drugs. When a child is exposed to such substances before birth, it can impact their neurological development, which in turn can affect their ability to form healthy and secure attachment relationships (Ross et al., 2015).

Related Conditions

Children with attachment disorders often experience difficulties across various domains of life, including academics, social interactions, emotional well-being, and behavior. These struggles can have a profound impact on their overall development and functioning.

Academically, children with attachment disorders may face challenges in a classroom setting. They may have difficulty concentrating, completing tasks, or following instructions. These difficulties can lead to lower academic performance and hinder their ability to reach their full potential.

Socially, children with attachment disorders may struggle to form and maintain healthy relationships with peers and adults. They may have difficulty trusting others, interpreting social cues, or regulating their emotions within social interactions. As a result, they may experience feelings of isolation or rejection and have limited social support networks.

Emotionally, children with attachment disorders may struggle with regulating their emotions. They may experience intense mood swings, have difficulty expressing their emotions appropriately, or have a limited range of emotional responses. These challenges can contribute to problems in managing stress, anxiety, and frustration, which can further impact their overall well-being.

Behaviorally, children with attachment disorders may exhibit disruptive or challenging behaviors. They may engage in impulsive or oppositional behaviors, have difficulty following rules or boundaries, or display aggression toward others. These behavioral challenges can create additional stressors within their family, school, and community environments.

Furthermore, children with attachment disorders are at a higher risk of encountering legal issues during adolescence (National Collaborating Centre for Mental Health [UK], 2015). Their struggles with emotional regulation, impulsivity, and difficulties with authority figures can increase their likelihood of engaging in delinquent behaviors or becoming involved in criminal activities.

In addition, children with attachment disorders may have lower IQ scores compared to their peers (Schröder et al., 2019). This cognitive impact can stem from a combination of genetic factors, environmental influences, and the impact of early adverse experiences on brain development. Furthermore, language problems are more prevalent among children with attachment disorders. They may have delays in language acquisition, difficulty with expressive or receptive language skills, or struggle to articulate their thoughts and ideas effectively.

Personality Disorders

It is important to understand that attachment disorders in children do not resolve on their own over time. While the symptoms may change or manifest differently as they transition into adulthood, they are likely to continue experiencing ongoing challenges if left untreated.

One significant aspect of attachment disorders that persists into adulthood is difficulty in regulating emotions. Individuals who have experienced attachment-related issues in childhood often struggle with managing their emotions effectively. They may have intense emotional reactions, find it challenging to control or express their feelings appropriately, or have difficulty identifying and understanding their emotional states. These difficulties in emotional regulation can lead to relationship problems, difficulties in managing stress, and overall emotional instability.

Furthermore, untreated attachment disorders can impact an individual's ability to form and maintain healthy relationships in adulthood. They may struggle with trust issues, fear of rejection or abandonment, and difficulty establishing intimate connections. These challenges can hinder the development of deep and secure relationships, preventing individuals from experiencing the support, closeness, and fulfillment that come with healthy attachments.

Additionally, untreated attachment disorders may have an impact on various aspects of an individual's life, including their mental health, academic or professional achievements, and overall well-being. The unresolved issues from childhood can contribute to increased vulnerability to mental health conditions such as anxiety, depression, or personality disorders. The lack of secure attachment experiences in childhood can also affect one's self-esteem, sense of identity, and ability to navigate life's challenges effectively.

Addressing attachment disorders and providing appropriate therapeutic interventions is essential for individuals to heal and develop healthier patterns of attachment. With the help of qualified professionals, individuals can work towards improving emotional regulation skills, building trust in relationships, and developing secure attachments. Through therapy, individuals can gain insights into the impact of their early attachment experiences, process any unresolved trauma, and learn healthier ways of relating to themselves and others.

It is crucial not to underestimate the long-lasting effects of untreated attachment disorders. Early intervention and ongoing support can make a significant difference in helping individuals overcome these challenges and cultivate healthier relationships, emotional well-being, and overall life satisfaction as they move into adulthood.

Chapter Summary

- Anxious attachment is a type of insecure relationship children have with mothers or caregivers.

- The type of attachment you had with your mother or primary caregiver can affect your relationships as an adult.

- There are four main attachment styles: secure, anxious-ambivalent, anxious-avoidant, and disorganized.

- Anxious attachment can make coping with stress and change difficult, affecting romantic and other relationships.

- Prevention and improvement strategies include learning communication skills, seeking therapy, and building relationships with securely attached individuals.

Chapter 2

Anxious Attachment & Relationships

"I think about you all the time. I hear your voice in my head, I rehearse conversations with you, I talk to myself, and imagine I'm talking to you. And I wish you felt like this about me, but I know you don't and I don't think you ever will. I think you're happy giving people your scraps. I think that's easy for you, and I don't blame you, because I hate being like this, and I wish I was more like you."

Eliza Clark.

Having an anxious attachment style can present challenges in relationships. Those with this attachment style are highly sensitive to their partner's needs and perceive them well. However, they also constantly need reassurance and affection to feel secure in their romantic relationship. If they don't receive the validation they seek, they can become worried and stressed about the state of their relationship.

Individuals with an anxious attachment style tend to internalize a perceived lack of affection and intimacy as a sign that they are not deserving of love. This leads to an intense fear of rejection. To avoid being abandoned, someone with an anxious attachment style may become clingy, hypervigilant, and prone to jealousy in their relationship. The fear of being alone overwhelms them, so they do everything they can to hold on to their partner. They see their partner as the solution to their deep emotional needs.

Recognizing Patterns

Individuals with an anxious attachment style often desire deep and meaningful connections in their romantic relationships. However, they also tend to experience high levels of stress and anxiety within these relationships. While they are highly attuned to their partner's needs and willing to go above and beyond to meet them, their insecurities and doubts about their self-worth can cause them to project their uncertainties onto their partner's behaviors. This means that if their partner does not always respond in the way they expect or meet their emotional needs, they perceive it as confirmation that they do not deserve love.

For someone with an anxious attachment style, relationships can be both a source of comfort and distress. On one hand, they have a deep fear of rejection and abandonment, which leads them to be hyper-vigilant and constantly on the lookout for any potential threat to the relationship. They constantly seek validation and reassurance from their partner, needing constant confirmation that they are loved. This constant need for reassurance can be exhausting for both parties involved. On the other hand, being in the presence of their loved one can offer them a sense of comfort and soothing, temporarily alleviating their anxiety.

Signs of an anxious attachment style in relationships include being highly attuned to their partner's needs and emotions, often prioritizing their partner's needs over their own, constantly seeking validation and assurance of their worthiness, being hyper-vigilant and overly sensitive to any perceived threats to the relationship, having a deep fear of rejection and abandonment, experiencing jealousy and suspicion towards their partner's actions, displaying clingy behavior and struggling with establishing healthy boundaries, finding it difficult to express and understand their own intense emotions, and experiencing excessive anxiety and worry about the relationship.

Ultimately, the traits associated with an anxious attachment style can be detrimental to one's love life, as they can trigger avoidant strategies in their partner, causing them to withdraw and distance themselves. Therefore, individuals with an anxious attachment style must recognize and manage their attachment patterns to cultivate healthy and fulfilling relationships.

Why Does This Happen?

Deep within, individuals with an anxious attachment style harbor a belief that once their partners truly get to know them, they will lose interest and reject them. This underlying fear stems from their low self-esteem, causing them to believe they are not good enough to maintain their partner's interest in the long run.

It is important to recognize that the thoughts and behaviors of someone with an anxious attachment style are deeply rooted in their childhood experiences. If their need for affection and intimacy is not met during their early years, it may shape their beliefs about themselves and their importance. Often, their needs were brushed aside or disregarded, leading them to believe that they and their needs were unimportant. As a result, they anticipate this pattern in their romantic relationships and go to great lengths to prevent it from happening again.

The anxious attacher's constant need for reassurance and validation is driven by their deep-seated fear of being insignificant and unlovable. They may constantly seek confirmation of their partner's love, fearing that any sign of distance or indifference signifies their impending rejection. Their actions are guided by their desperate efforts to avoid abandonment, as they believe their self-worth depends entirely on their ability to sustain a partner's interest and affection.

Understanding the origins of their anxious attachment style can provide insight into why they think and act the way they do in relationships. By acknowledging and addressing these deep-rooted insecurities, individuals with an anxious attachment style can develop healthier attachment patterns, build self-esteem, and nurture more secure and fulfilling connections with their partners.

Forming Healthy Relationships

Managing an anxious attachment style in relationships can be challenging due to the deeply ingrained patterns of attachment anxiety. However, with understanding and consistent effort, navigating and overcoming the deep-rooted fears and insecurities associated with this attachment style is possible, leading to a more fulfilling and secure romantic partnership.

A crucial step in managing an anxious attachment style is understanding the events or actions that trigger attachment insecurity. By identifying these triggers, individuals with an anxious attachment style can gain insight into how their thoughts and actions are influenced, allowing them to develop strategies to counter their typical negative responses.

Common triggers for individuals with an anxious attachment style in relationships include situations where a partner acts distant or aloof, forgets important events like anniversaries, behaves in a friendly or flirtatious manner with someone else, comes home late, or fails to respond to messages and calls promptly, and fails to compliment changes such as new clothes or a new hairstyle. Any of these triggers can potentially lead the anxious attacher to feel overwhelmed by worry or fear of rejection.

When triggered, the attachment system of someone with an anxious attachment style may activate, leading them to respond to the perceived threat to the relationship by seeking as much closeness with their partner as possible, excessively worrying, and feeling emotionally depleted. Although driven by a genuine desire for security and reassurance, these behaviors can strain a relationship and even lead to a breakup.

To manage an anxious attachment style, individuals can work on developing healthier coping mechanisms and communication skills. This may involve practicing self-soothing techniques to calm anxiety, challenging negative thoughts and insecurities, setting and maintaining healthy boundaries, and expressing their needs and concerns openly and effectively to their partner. Additionally, engaging in self-care, building self-esteem, and seeking therapy or support can be beneficial in addressing the underlying issues associated with an anxious attachment style.

It is important to remember that managing an anxious attachment style in relationships is an ongoing process that requires patience, self-awareness, and consistent effort. With time and dedication, individuals with an anxious attachment style can create more secure and satisfying relationships, breaking free from the negative cycles of anxiety and insecurity.

Effective Communication

An individual with an anxious attachment style often struggles with managing their negative emotions. They may react to their partner through bursts of anger or jealousy in an attempt to regain closeness or address their insecurities. Effective communication is important in these situations, involving taking a moment to reflect on emotions before taking action. Expressing the reasons behind frustration or worry can help open a conversation with your partner.

Loving someone with an anxious attachment style means understanding their intense fear of rejection and abandonment. This fear stems from feelings of unworthiness and can lead to a hyper-focus on any perceived threats to the relationship. Anxious individuals may exhibit protest behaviors. Protest behavior is when you're seeking validation from your partner by engaging in unhealthy behavior. This leads to self-criticism and lower self-esteem. Dealing with an anxious attachment partner can be challenging, but it is important to have an open and clear discussion about their needs and boundaries in the relationship. As I move ahead in the book, I will speak more about communication and how to improve it.

Consistency is crucial for someone with an anxious attachment style. Reassure them of their importance to you and let them know you are there to support them. Allowing your partner to express their anxieties can help them recognize any irrational thought patterns. Validate their emotions and challenge the negative narratives by providing evidence to the contrary. It is important to remember that attachment styles can be changed with knowledge, understanding, and the right tools.

Individuals with an anxious attachment style can develop a "learned" secure attachment by identifying and addressing irrational thoughts about themselves and their relationships. This can be achieved through different approaches, such as therapy, discussions with a partner or trusted friend, or by using workbooks. Regardless of the approach, consistent effort is key to achieving meaningful change. It's also important to understand how your partner can help in situations like these.

How Attachment Manifests

Anxious attachment can manifest in various ways in relationships. Here are a few examples:

- **Constant need for reassurance:** Someone with an anxious attachment may constantly seek reassurance and validation from their partner. They may crave reassurances about their partner's love and commitment, often seeking verbal confirmation of their partner's feelings.

- **Overanalyzing and overthinking behaviors:** People with an anxious attachment tend to overanalyze every action and word in a relationship, attaching meaning to even the smallest details. They may often question their partner's intentions or read into their behaviors more than necessary, leading to unnecessary conflicts or misunderstandings.

- **Fear of abandonment:** Individuals with anxious attachment often have a deep-seated fear of being abandoned. They may worry excessively about their partner leaving them, even when no evidence supports such fears. This fear can lead to clingy behavior and an inability to give their partner space.

- **Overdependence on the relationship:** People with anxious attachment tend to rely heavily on their partner for their emotional well-being. They may have difficulty being independent and often struggle with their own sense of self. This can create an imbalanced dynamic where they rely on their partner for their happiness, potentially leading to feelings of neediness or codependency.

- **Jealousy and possessiveness:** Anxious attachment can also manifest as jealousy and possessiveness in relationships. Due to their insecurity and fear of losing their partner, individuals with an anxious attachment may become overly possessive or jealous when it comes to their partner's interactions with others, even if there is no reason to suspect infidelity.

Remember, attachment styles are not set in stone, and individuals may display a combination of attachment behaviors from different styles. It is important for individuals with anxious attachment to build their self-esteem, cultivate trust, and develop healthy communication skills to foster more secure and fulfilling relationships.

Overcoming Attachment Challenges

John and Mary were deeply in love with each other. However, they both struggled with anxious attachment in their relationship, which caused frequent misunderstandings, insecurities, and a constant need for reassurance.

John had grown up in a family where his parents were inconsistent in their affection and emotional availability. Consequently, he developed an anxious attachment style and always sought validation from his partners. Mary, on the other hand, had experienced a traumatic breakup in the past, leading her to become hypersensitive to any signs of rejection or abandonment.

Their anxieties often manifested in different ways. John would constantly bombard Mary with text messages and calls, seeking reassurance of her love and commitment. Mary, overwhelmed by his constant need for validation, would occasionally withdraw to protect herself from potential rejection.

One day, they decided to confront their attachment challenges head-on. They realized that their anxieties were driving them apart and hindering the growth of their relationship. With courage and determination, they embarked on a journey of healing and growth.

John and Mary sought support from a counselor who specialized in attachment styles. The counselor helped them understand the roots of their anxieties and provided them with the necessary tools to overcome them. They learned the importance of open communication, setting healthy boundaries, and building self-confidence.

As they worked together, John and Mary gradually started to weaken the grip of their anxious attachment style. They now focused on building trust, embracing vulnerability, and practicing mindfulness in their relationship. They learned to express their needs and fears without overwhelming each other, creating a safe and secure environment for growth.

In time, their relationship transformed. John's constant need for reassurance slowly waned, and Mary's fears of abandonment lessened. They began to find strength within themselves and their partnership, realizing they were both worthy of love and that their anxious attachment did not define them.

If you also feel like John or Mary and have similar things happening in your own relationship, rest assured that you are not alone. This book will equip you with tools and information to not only understand your attachment better but also help you overcome it.

Impact on Relationships

Our early relationships with our parents or primary caregivers form the foundation for how we perceive and interact with relationships as we grow older. As we transition into late childhood and adolescence, our peer relationships become increasingly important and further shape our attachment style. Eventually, these experiences with peers impact how we enter into romantic relationships, which in turn continues to shape our attachment style. However, it's important to note that while our early experiences significantly impact our attachment style, they are not the sole determinants. Other factors also contribute, and our attachment style can change over time.

In general, individuals with a secure attachment style have had their needs consistently met during infancy. They grow up with a sense of competence and are comfortable acknowledging their limitations. As adults, they have healthy boundaries, can communicate their needs effectively in their relationships, and are not afraid to end unhealthy relationships when necessary.

On the other hand, individuals with an anxious attachment style have received love and care in an inconsistent manner during infancy. They tend to have a positive view of others but a negative view of themselves. In their romantic relationships, they often idealize their partner and heavily rely on them for their self-esteem. This can lead to behaviors such as making numerous phone calls in a short period when their partner doesn't answer.

Different attachment styles tend to manifest in predictable ways within intimate relationships. Secure individuals can navigate relationships with both anxious and avoidant types. They are comfortable enough with themselves to provide the reassurance that anxious types need while also giving avoidant types the space they require without feeling threatened.

Interestingly, anxious and avoidant individuals often find themselves in relationships with each other more frequently than with their own attachment type (Mark Manson, 2021). This may seem counterintuitive, but there is a reason behind it. Avoidant types are skilled at keeping others at a distance, and it is often the persistent efforts of anxious types that lead to these avoidant individuals opening up in a relationship.

Signs of an Anxiously Attached Partner

Seeking Assurance Repeatedly

Anxiously attached partners place a great deal of importance on their relationships as a means of validating their self-worth, feeling safe and secure, and defining their identity. This preoccupation with the relationship often leads to a constant state of worry (Lebow, 2022).

To seek reassurance, individuals with an anxious attachment style may resort to behaviors such as bombarding their partner with numerous texts or voicemails if they don't receive a prompt response. They may become anxious or upset if their partner appears distant, critical, or unhappy, constantly analyzing their partner's actions and words to decipher hidden meanings.

Moreover, those with an anxious attachment style frequently seek compliments and acknowledgment, constantly requiring reassurance from their partner that they are loved and will not be abandoned. Unfortunately, this incessant need for reassurance and validation can overwhelm their partner, as it may feel like they are being burdened with excessive or unreasonable demands.

The behavior of an anxiously attached partner, driven by their need for reassurance and validation, often creates tension and strain in the relationship. Their partner may struggle to meet the constant need for reassurance, leading to frustration and being overwhelmed. It is crucial for individuals with an anxious attachment style to establish boundaries and find healthier ways to manage their anxiety and need for validation to cultivate more balanced and fulfilling relationships.

Crave Closeness

Anxiously attached partners often find it challenging to regulate and soothe their emotions. They tend to look outside themselves for solutions to their internal struggles, believing their feelings can only be resolved through their relationships. However, relying solely on external sources for emotional stability is not sustainable.

Individuals with an anxious attachment style may experience a range of concerns and anxieties within their relationships. They may constantly worry that intimacy is not genuine or that it won't last, leading to a sense of insecurity and doubt about the authenticity of the connection. Even when things are going well in the relationship, they find it difficult to fully relax or enjoy the positive moments, as there is a constant fear that the good times will eventually come to an end.

Furthermore, anxiously attached partners tend to become more anxious when times are good, as they anticipate their partner will eventually grow tired of them or lose interest. They are hyper-vigilant for any signs that their partner may be pulling away or losing affection, which further fuels their anxiety.

The impact of an anxiously attached partner's difficulty in trusting is significant. Their partner may make sincere efforts to help them build trust, offering reassurances and demonstrating their commitment. However, over time, despite their best intentions, the anxiously attached partner may come to believe that their partner's efforts will never be enough to alleviate their deep-rooted insecurities. This can create a sense of frustration and helplessness in both partners, as the anxiously attached partner's persistent doubts and fears continue to undermine the trust and stability of the relationship.

In order to develop healthier patterns within their relationships, individuals with an anxious attachment need to focus on developing trust and security within themselves. This involves learning to regulate their emotions, cultivating self-compassion, and building a sense of inner security independent of external validation. With time and deliberate effort, it is possible for anxiously attached partners to develop more secure attachment styles and establish more fulfilling and balanced relationships.

Sabotaging a Relationship

People with anxious attachment often have a deep fear of not being able to cope without their partner. This fear can manifest in various ways, and one common response is to unconsciously push their partner away to cope with the underlying fear of their partner pulling away.

Anxiously attached individuals may exhibit behaviors such as jealousy or possessiveness. They may constantly worry that their partner will be attracted to someone else or will find someone better, leading them to become excessively possessive or territorial in their relationship. This behavior stems from their deep-seated fear of abandonment and a need for constant reassurance that their partner is committed to them.

Another way anxiously attached individuals may cope with their fears is by testing their partner's love or loyalty. They may intentionally create situations that provoke their partner's reaction, looking for signs that their partner truly cares for them. This testing behavior stems from a need for constant validation and reassurance that their partner's love is genuine.

In addition, anxiously attached individuals may engage in complaining or nitpicking. They may constantly find faults in their partner or the relationship, often as a means to seek attention or reassurance. By highlighting these perceived flaws, they seek validation that their partner is committed and willing to address their concerns.

In extreme cases, anxiously attached individuals may engage in stalking or harassment behaviors. Their fear of losing their partner can lead them to monitor their partner's activities excessively or invade their privacy. These behaviors can stem from an overwhelming need to maintain control and ensure their partner is always available and committed to them.

Lastly, anxiously attached individuals may become despondent or argumentative when their partner expresses a desire for solo activities or alone time. They may feel threatened or rejected by their partner's need for independence and interpret it as a sign that their partner is pulling away. This can manifest as emotional outbursts, clinginess, or attempts to guilt trip their partner into spending more time with them.

The possessiveness exhibited by anxiously attached partners significantly impacts their relationship. Their partner may feel constantly under scrutiny and mistrusted, causing strain and a lack of emotional safety within the relationship. The anxiously attached partner's possessive behavior can create a sense of suffocation and hinder the growth of trust and intimacy in the relationship.

Working on developing secure attachment and addressing underlying fears and insecurities is crucial for individuals with anxious attachment styles. By cultivating self-confidence and practicing effective communication, anxiously attached individuals can learn to manage their fears and build healthier, more trusting relationships.

Seeking to be Perfect

Anxiously attached partners often fear not being loved or accepted for who they truly are. They believe they can only receive love and approval if they constantly act in a way considered "perfect" or "best." This means hiding their vulnerable side and only showing their partner the parts of themselves that they believe will be liked and accepted. They are afraid that if their partner sees their true selves, with all their flaws and insecurities, they will be rejected.

Because of this fear, anxiously attached partners may believe that their love and value in the relationship depends on what they do for their partner rather than who they are as a person. They may feel that as long as they can fulfill their partner's needs and desires, they will be loved. This can lead to a lot of pressure and anxiety for the anxiously attached partner, as they constantly feel the need to go above and beyond to keep the relationship intact.

Anxiously attached partners also tend to feel responsible for maintaining the relationship and preventing it from falling apart. They may feel it is solely their job to cater to their partner's needs and make them happy. This can lead to feelings of resentment towards their partner, as they may feel that their efforts are not being reciprocated. They may silently expect their partner to do as much for them as they do for their partner, but they hesitate to express these feelings directly.

In their eagerness to please their partner, anxiously attached partners often neglect their own needs. They may engage in people-pleasing behaviors, constantly putting their partner's needs before their own. They may also have loose boundaries, allowing their partner to cross personal boundaries without speaking up. They may try to be indispensable to their partner, believing that their worth in the relationship is dependent on how much they can do for their partner.

As a result of these behaviors, anxiously attached partners may find themselves accepting unhealthy treatment from their partners. They may tolerate behaviors that are harmful or disrespectful because they believe that this is what it takes to keep their partner's love and approval. They may also hesitate to ask for what they need directly, fearing that their partner will be upset or reject them for having needs of their own.

The consequence of anxiously attached partners constantly striving to appear perfect and meet their partner's every need is that their partner may assume everything is fine in the relationship. Their partner may believe that the anxiously attached partner is happy and fulfilled because they are always trying their best to please. However, when the anxiously attached partner finally can no longer bear the weight of their own suppressed needs and resentments, they may explode with complaints and grievances seemingly out of nowhere. This can be confusing and blindsiding for their partner, who may have been unaware of the anxiously attached partner's inner struggles.

Live in Emotional Turmoil

Anxiously attached partners are sensitive to their emotions, unlike avoidantly attached individuals who tend to suppress their feelings. They often experience intense emotions of loneliness, emptiness, or a lack of safety in their relationships. These emotions can be overwhelming and may lead the anxiously attached partner to exhibit certain behaviors and patterns.

As a result of their fear of abandonment, anxiously attached partners may also have frequent or dramatic emotional ups and downs. They can easily become overwhelmed by their emotions and may react exaggeratedly to seemingly small triggers. Their emotions can be intense and quickly fluctuate, making it difficult for them to maintain a sense of emotional stability. They may often feel overwhelmed by their emotions and struggle to regulate or control them.

Another characteristic of anxiously attached partners is their tendency to create drama in their relationships. This can manifest in various ways, such as starting arguments or engaging in attention-seeking behaviors. They may unconsciously create conflict in order to seek reassurance or attention from their partner. This constant drama can be exhausting for the anxiously attached partner and their partner, creating a cycle of emotional turbulence and strain in the relationship.

The consequence of an anxiously attached partner's heightened emotionality is that their partner may feel smothered or exhausted. The intense need for reassurance and constant emotional fluctuations can be overwhelming for their partner. The anxiously attached partner's fear of abandonment may result in them being overly clingy or possessive, which can feel suffocating and restrictive for their partner. The constant drama and emotional rollercoaster may drain their partner's energy and make them feel like they are always walking on eggshells.

Feeling One-Down

Individuals with an anxious attachment style often carry deep-seated insecurities and fears related to their self-worth and desirability. They may constantly question their value and worry that something inherently wrong with them pushes people away. These feelings of being unlovable, powerless, alone, and undesirable can create a constant state of anxiety and insecurity in their relationships.

As a result of these insecurities, anxiously attached partners often project their fears and doubts onto their partners. They may misinterpret innocent actions or harmless remarks from their partner as indicators that their partner doesn't truly care for them or is planning to leave. Even the smallest signs of distance or perceived rejection can trigger intense anxiety and self-doubt in the anxiously attached partner.

This tendency to misconstrue their partner's intentions and misinterpret their actions can create a significant burden for their partner. The anxiously attached partner's constant need for reassurance and validation can make their partner feel responsible for their happiness and emotional well-being. They may feel burdened by the pressure to constantly prove their love and commitment to their anxious partner, as any perceived lapse in attention or affection can be exaggerated and lead to feelings of rejection.

The anxiously attached partner's one-down stance, fueled by their fears of being unlovable and undesirable, can create a dynamic where their partner feels responsible for managing their partner's emotions and happiness (Psychology Today, n.d.). A one-down stance in a relationship refers to a position where one person consistently puts themselves in a lower or subordinate position compared to their partner. This can manifest in behaviors such as constantly checking in, praising and reassuring their partner, and making sacrifices to meet their partner's needs, even at the expense of their well-being.

Over time, this dynamic can become exhausting and overwhelming for the partner of an anxiously attached individual. They may feel constant pressure to prove their love and support, which can lead to feelings of resentment and frustration. The anxiously attached partner's dependency on their partner for validation and reassurance can leave the partner feeling emotionally drained and burdened by the weight of their partner's unhappiness.

Overinvesting in the Relationship

Individuals with an anxious attachment style have a strong desire for deep and meaningful connections in their relationships. They may enter a new partnership, hoping to finally fulfill their longing for intimacy and closeness. However, this intense longing and need for connection can manifest in various behaviors and patterns within the relationship that can strain both partners.

Anxiously attached individuals often seek rapid emotional intimacy and may try to accelerate the pace of the relationship. They may feel an urgency to establish a deep bond with their partner and may push for the relationship to progress quickly, bypassing the natural progression of getting to know each other at a more gradual pace.

To quell their anxieties and uncertainties, anxiously attached partners frequently seek reassurance and validation from their partners. They may constantly ask their partner about the state of the relationship, seeking confirmation that their partner values and cares for them. However, this constant need for reassurance can be emotionally exhausting for the partner and may create feelings of suffocation or being overwhelmed.

In addition, anxiously attached partners may overly idealize their partner or the relationship itself. They might place their partner on a pedestal and see them as perfect or view the relationship as flawless. This idealization can serve as a defense mechanism that shields them from their fears of rejection or abandonment. However, it can also create unrealistic expectations and lead to disappointment or frustration when the partner inevitably falls short of the idealized image.

The fixation on the relationship that characterizes anxiously attached individuals can consume their time and attention. They may become preoccupied with the relationship, constantly thinking about it and investing significant energy and effort into maintaining it. This intense focus on the relationship can sometimes cause them to neglect other important aspects of their life, such as personal hobbies, friendships, or career goals.

The consequence of an anxiously attached partner's overwhelming focus on the relationship is that their partner may feel burdened with responsibilities they didn't sign up for or feel capable of fulfilling. The constant need for reassurance, the rapid advancement of the relationship, and the idealization can create a heavy emotional weight on their partner's shoulders. They may feel overwhelmed by the pressure to meet the anxiously attached partner's emotional needs and live up to their expectations.

The relentless fixation on the relationship by the anxiously attached partner can leave their partner feeling trapped or suffocated, as if their own needs and desires are overshadowed by the demands of the relationship. This imbalance can lead to strain and difficulties in maintaining a healthy and fulfilling partnership for both individuals involved.

Helping Your Partner

If you find yourself in a relationship with a partner who has an anxious attachment style, it can be challenging to navigate how to provide them with the support they need while also maintaining your own independence. It is important to seek your own support during this time, but some strategies can help you support your partner with anxious attachment.

First and foremost, it is beneficial to identify your attachment style and how it may influence the dynamics of the relationship. For example, if you have an avoidant attachment style, you may find it difficult to meet your partner's needs for closeness. Understanding your attachment style can provide insight into your own behaviors and help you be more compassionate towards your partner's anxieties.

Clear and effective communication is crucial when supporting a partner with an anxious attachment. It is important to be direct and empathetic when talking to your partner about your needs and boundaries. For instance, if you are unable to message your partner during the workday, it is important to clearly communicate this to them. Being vague about your boundaries can lead to miscommunication and unnecessary worry for your partner.

Establishing consistency and connection in the relationship can also provide support to a partner with an anxious attachment. Creating routines that allow both you and your partner to feel connected and valued can be incredibly helpful. This could involve setting aside a specific night each week for a date, enjoying a cup of coffee together before work, or simply sending each other a text before going to bed. While maintaining consistency won't necessarily change your partner's attachment style, it can create a stable foundation where healing can occur.

It is important to note that attachment styles can change over time. A person with an anxious attachment style may begin to feel more secure and safe with a committed and emotionally available partner. This means that the effects of anxious attachment may become less invasive in long-term relationships. Healthy relationships that prioritize clear communication and mutual respect can help reshape your attachment style and provide you with new experiences that contradict any negative childhood experiences tied to attachment.

Dating Tips

To successfully navigate the initial stages of dating and find a healthy match for yourself, it is crucial to have self-awareness and take specific steps to manage your anxious attachment style. Alongside being aware of your attachment style, here are some tips to help you navigate dating:

Recognize when you are overly preoccupied with the relationship in your mind. This could manifest as frequently imagining a future together or constantly replaying past conversations in your head. While some level of thinking about the relationship is normal, excessive or intrusive thoughts can hinder your ability to fully engage with the present. Acknowledge when this occurs and label it for what it is: intrusive thoughts.

Redirect your attention to your immediate environment. When you notice yourself spiraling into thoughts about the relationship, deliberately shift your focus to what is happening in the present moment. Engage in activities or conversations that keep you grounded and centered. By redirecting your attention, you can break the cycle of anxious rumination and regain a sense of balance and presence.

Practice mindfulness techniques. Mindfulness involves intentionally paying attention to the present moment without judgment. It can be useful in managing anxiety and helping you stay grounded. Engage in mindfulness techniques such as deep breathing exercises, meditation, or guided imagery to bring yourself back to the present and reduce anxious thoughts.

Communicate your needs and concerns. It is important to communicate openly and honestly with your partner about your anxious attachment style and any concerns or insecurities you may have. By expressing your needs and fears, you can foster a sense of emotional safety and understanding in the relationship. Effective communication can help both partners navigate uncertainties and build a stronger foundation.

Take things at a comfortable pace. It is crucial not to rush into a committed relationship or put undue pressure on yourself or your partner. Allow the relationship to evolve naturally and take time to build trust and connection. Setting healthy boundaries and being mindful of your emotional well-being is essential. This allows you and your partner to feel secure and develop a solid foundation for a healthy relationship.

When you sense that something is not quite right in a new dating relationship, it is essential to pause before reacting. The initial instinct may be to hurry and reconnect with the person, seeking reassurance or clarification about the situation. However, it is important to step back and check in with yourself before acting impulsively.

Take a moment to acknowledge and identify your feelings. Are you feeling anxious, insecure, or uncertain about the relationship? Recognize that your emotions can be heightened by your anxious attachment style. Validate your feelings and remind yourself that it is normal to have some level of unease in the early stages of dating.

Instead of immediately seeking validation from your partner, shift your focus inward. Take steps to soothe yourself and calm your nervous system. Engage in activities that bring you comfort and relaxation, such as deep breathing, meditation, or a hobby you enjoy. This self-soothing exercise will help regulate your emotions and allow you to approach the situation with a clear and more grounded mindset.

Reframe your perspective on the need for immediate connection. Rather than feeling the urgency to reconnect with your partner right away, recognize that what you truly need is to regain a sense of calm and equilibrium within yourself. By prioritizing self-care and emotional well-being, you can approach the relationship from a place of inner strength and stability.

Remember that taking time to self-soothe and reflect does not mean neglecting the relationship or avoiding difficult conversations. It simply means recognizing that your immediate need is to center yourself before engaging with your partner. This pause can actually benefit the relationship by allowing you to respond in a more thoughtful and balanced manner.

Chapter Summary

- The Anxious attachment style is characterized by high sensitivity to a partner's needs and a constant need for reassurance and affection.

- Individuals with this attachment style internalize a lack of affection as a sign that they do not deserve love, leading to intense fear of rejection.

- To avoid abandonment, those with anxious attachment may become clingy, hypervigilant, and prone to jealousy in relationships.

- Anxious individuals see their partner as the solution to their emotional needs and fear of being alone.

- Lack of validation and reassurance can cause worry and stress for those with an anxious attachment style in their romantic relationships.

Chapter 3

Links to Your Past

"Learn from past experiences but accept them all as perfect while staying in the present. Let go of everything that doesn't serve you."
Mike Basevic.

Various factors, including genetic components and early childhood experiences, can trigger anxious attachment. Research has shown that anxiety tends to have a genetic component, with children as young as four months of age displaying behavioral disinhibition that is linked to later separation anxiety (Madrid, 2012).

However, childhood experiences can also contribute to attachment anxiety. For instance, being raised by overprotective parents, experiencing abuse or neglect can result in insecure attachment patterns. Attachment plays a critical role in ensuring a child's survival as it establishes a sense of security for the child. For instance, when a child experiences distress, their instinct is to seek comfort from their attachment figures.

If a child fails to receive comforting responses from the attachment figures, they may not develop a sense of security. This can lead to elevated levels of fear, anxiety, and distress that linger throughout life. This pattern can repeat itself in later relationships, where the individual may expect comfort from others but fail to receive it, leading to feelings of insecurity and further perpetuating negative attachment patterns.

Coping With Anxious Attachment

Individuals with attachment anxiety often resort to ineffective coping strategies, such as excessive checking on their partner, which only exacerbates their anxiety and strains their relationships. Identifying helpful and healthy coping strategies to break free from these negative patterns is crucial.

If you recognize signs of anxious attachment in your behavior, there are several strategies you can implement to manage these tendencies and improve your overall well-being:

Being mindful of your partner's attachment style can help in understanding how it affects your attachment anxiety. A partner with a secure attachment style can provide a stable and nurturing environment, fostering a more secure attachment for both individuals. Try to foster open and honest communication with your partner. Encourage them to express their feelings, fears, and needs without judgment. Create a safe space where they can share their thoughts and experiences. Also, listen attentively to your partner and try to understand their perspective. Validate their emotions and show empathy. Also, try being responsive and available to your partner's emotional needs. Offer reassurance and support when they express anxiety or insecurity.

Instead of dwelling on past negative experiences, consciously make new choices that align with your desired life. Shifting your perspective towards a positive future can help reduce attachment anxiety.

Let's look at a short story. Emma realized that she had to make new choices to create the life she truly desired. She began by looking closer at her current situation and identifying what was holding her back.

Emma discovered that fear and self-doubt were the main culprits preventing her from taking risks and pursuing her passions. But she was determined to change that. One by one, Emma started making choices that aligned with her goals. She left her unfulfilling job and pursued a career in a field she was passionate about. She made a conscious effort to surround herself with positive and supportive individuals who believed in her dreams.

Emma also prioritized her self-care. She made time for exercise, meditation, and activities that brought her joy. As her physical and mental well-being improved, so did her ability to make choices that aligned with her desired life.

Working with a therapist experienced in helping individuals transition from insecure to secure attachment can be immensely beneficial. Through therapy, you can gain insights into your attachment patterns, explore underlying causes, and learn effective strategies to develop a more secure attachment style. A counselor or therapist can help in various situations.

Writing down your thoughts, feelings, and reactions in a journal provides a valuable outlet for self-reflection. This practice can help you gain a deeper understanding of your attachment anxiety and identify patterns or triggers that contribute to it. Try doing this every day, to begin with, and eventually do it once a week.

Learn more about attachment anxiety to enhance your understanding of the issue. This knowledge can empower you to make informed choices, alter your perspective, and develop healthier coping mechanisms. This book is your companion in your healing journey. You may often come back to revisit the concepts and get ideas on what to do to reduce your relationship anxiety.

Recognize the people in your life who tend to trigger your attachment anxiety. When you interact with certain people, pay attention to how you feel. Do you feel anxious, worried, or insecure? Acknowledge these emotions and their intensity. Look for consistent patterns in your emotional responses. Are there specific people who consistently make you feel anxious or trigger your attachment anxiety? This awareness allows you to proactively manage your responses and set boundaries to minimize anxiety-inducing situations.

Coping With an Anxious Partner

If you are in a relationship with someone who has attachment anxiety, there are ways you can support and help them feel more secure:

- **Validate their feelings:** Acknowledging and validating your partner's feelings is crucial rather than minimizing or dismissing them. Don't shut them out. Rather than saying, "You're suffocating me," try saying, "I understand what you're going through, and I want to help you." Understanding that their attachment anxiety is real and significant can make a significant difference in their sense of security.

- **Communication and awareness:** Encourage open communication about how their attachment anxiety affects your relationship. By discussing this together, both partners can better understand triggers, patterns, and potential solutions. As mentioned in the previous point, speak with them and understand their feelings rather than shutting them out.

- **Consistency and reliability:** Building trust is essential for someone with attachment anxiety. Be consistent in your words and actions, honoring commitments and promises. This consistency helps reassure your partner that they can rely on you and fosters a more secure attachment. Something as simple as sharing your phone's password with your partner shows that you trust them.

- **Show care and reassurance regularly:** Make an effort to demonstrate your care and concern for your partner on a regular basis. Small gestures of love and affection, kind words, and reassurance can go a long way in alleviating their attachment anxiety.

- **Couples therapy:** Consider attending couples therapy together. This can be an effective approach to addressing attachment-related issues as a couple, improving communication and understanding, and finding constructive ways to manage attachment anxiety within the relationship. A therapist can facilitate discussions, provide tools, and help both partners develop healthier attachment patterns.

Remember to approach these strategies with empathy, patience, and understanding. Supporting a partner with attachment anxiety requires compassion, active listening, and a willingness to learn and grow together. By offering this support, you can contribute to creating a more secure and fulfilling relationship for both of you.

Getting Over Your Past

Those with an anxious attachment style often carry emotional baggage from their past, particularly from experiences with their parents or significant romantic relationships. If their parents were consistently inattentive to their emotional or physical needs or if they were let down in previous relationships, it can lead to the development of an anxious attachment style.

The lessons we learned in our formative years can shape our behavior and coping strategies in our current relationships. However, sometimes, these once-helpful strategies can become counterproductive. For example, you may attempt to protect yourself by controlling or worrying about outcomes, but such behaviors can harm your relationships.

To address this, it is necessary to heal and let go of past disappointments so that you can accurately assess and respond to the present situation. When you have an anxious attachment style, it can be challenging to differentiate between your reactions and the role your partner plays in the dynamic.

To uncover the influence of your past on your current relationships, consider whether there are any similarities between your current experiences and what you went through as a child or witnessed in your parents' relationship. This self-reflection can help shed light on how your attachment style manifests in your current interactions.

Ask yourself, "What can I learn from my past?" Reflect on the lessons or insights that your experiences have given you. Consider how it has shaped your perspective, values, or decision-making.

By acknowledging the impact of your past experiences and recognizing how they may be affecting your present relationships, you can begin the process of healing and working towards a more secure attachment style. It may be helpful to seek the support of a therapist who specializes in attachment-related issues. They can guide you on this journey of self-discovery and provide tools to develop healthier patterns in your relationships. With time, effort, and self-compassion, you can free yourself from the limitations of anxious attachment and cultivate more fulfilling and secure relationships.

Focused Exercises

To delve deeper into the link between childhood experiences and your current anxious attachment style, below are some detailed exercises you can try. Give yourself permission to take it at your own pace and be patient with yourself as you navigate this journey of understanding and healing your anxious attachment style.

- **Reflect on your early childhood experiences:** Set aside some dedicated time to reflect on your relationship with your primary caregivers during your early years. Consider aspects such as the consistency of care you received, how responsive they were to your needs, and whether you felt secure and loved. Write down any significant memories or patterns that come to mind, noting positive and challenging experiences.

- **Identify attachment-related triggers:** Pay close attention to situations or behaviors that trigger your anxious attachment style. Take note of instances where you feel a heightened need for reassurance or become overly sensitive to your partner's actions. Sensory experiences such as specific smells, tastes, sounds, or tactile sensations can trigger memories or emotions associated with the trauma. Write down these triggers and try to identify any common themes or patterns that emerge. Understanding your triggers can help you become more aware of when your anxious attachment tendencies are activated.

- **Engage in journaling exercises:** Make journaling a regular practice to explore your attachment-related emotions and thoughts. Set aside dedicated time to write about specific incidents or conflicts that have triggered your anxious attachment style. Reflect on how you felt during those moments and explore any underlying fears or insecurities that arise. This process can help you gain insights into your emotional patterns and clarify what triggers your anxious attachments. At this step, it is recommended that you write in a physical journal, even though a digital journal is also possible. Set aside your phone, sit alone without distractions, take the time, feel the pen in your fingers, and truly focus on writing down your thoughts and feelings.

- **Practice self-compassion:** Cultivate self-compassion as a countermeasure to the negative beliefs and self-worth issues often associated with anxious attachment. When you experience feelings of anxiety or fear in your relationship, remind yourself that these emotions are natural responses rooted in your early experiences. Start by becoming aware of your thoughts, emotions, and physical sensations. Notice when you are being self-critical or judgmental towards yourself. Mindfulness helps you observe your experiences without getting caught up in them. This practice can help you challenge negative self-talk and develop a more compassionate and understanding perspective towards yourself.

Breaking Down Personal Patterns

Understanding and addressing personal patterns related to anxious attachment is a complex but crucial endeavor that can lead to personal growth and healthier relationships.

Use the knowledge from this book to learn more about anxious attachment styles and how they influence relationships. This will help you gain insights into your own patterns and behaviors. This could include identifying common triggers, reactions, or fears that tend to arise.

Anxious attachment often involves negative self-perception and a fear of abandonment. To break free from these patterns, actively work on challenging and reframing these negative thoughts and beliefs. Try using affirmations like "I deserve love and security in my relationships" or "I trust in the strength of my connections and believe in the goodness of others."

Identifying Triggers and Responses

Developing an understanding of your triggers and responses in relation to anxious attachment is a valuable process that can lead to greater self-awareness and the ability to manage your attachment style effectively.

When you experience triggers, it may feel as though you are reliving a traumatic event. However, a technique called the flashback halting protocol can help interrupt the flashback and bring you back to the present moment. This process can assist your mind and body in recognizing that the trauma is no longer happening.

Here's a detailed breakdown of the steps involved in the flashback halting protocol:

- **Recognize your current emotions:** Begin by acknowledging and labeling the emotions you are feeling at that moment. It could be fear, anxiety, panic, sadness, or any other emotion that arises during the flashback.

- **Observe the sensations in your body:** Take a moment to notice and identify any physical sensations you are experiencing. This could include shaking, sweating, dizziness, or other bodily responses associated with the triggering event.

- **Identify the trigger:** Identify the specific aspect of the traumatic event you remember or are reminded of. For instance, this could be the person involved, a particular vehicle, or a childhood-related memory.

- **Ground yourself in the present:** Shift your attention to the present by stating the current date and time. This helps remind your mind that the present moment is separate from the past trauma.

- **Recognize your environment:** Look around and identify five objects that you can see in your surroundings. Naming these objects engages your senses and brings your awareness to the present moment.

Practical Strategies for Breaking Negative Cycles

Breaking negative, anxious attachment cycles can be challenging, but with perseverance and the right strategies, it is possible to overcome them. Here are some strategies you can try to help break negative cycles. Start by focusing on your thoughts and identifying any negative, self-critical, or irrational patterns. Write them down and challenge them by asking yourself if they are based on evidence or if there are alternative perspectives to consider.

When negative thoughts arise, imagine how you would respond to a friend in a similar situation and offer yourself the same compassion. Create a list of positive affirmations or self-statements and repeat them daily. These affirmations can help counteract negative thoughts and build self-confidence.

When you catch yourself making negative assumptions or jumping to conclusions, challenge those interpretations by considering alternative explanations or seeking evidence to support or refute your assumptions. Try asking yourself, "Why did this happen?" rather than "This shouldn't have happened."

Chapter Summary

- Anxious attachment can be triggered by genetic components and early childhood experiences.

- Genes play a role in anxiety, with children displaying behavioral disinhibition at a young age that later leads to separation anxiety.

- Childhood experiences, such as overprotective parenting, abuse, and neglect, can contribute to insecure attachment patterns.

- Attachment is crucial for a child's survival as it establishes a sense of security and comfort.

- If a child does not receive comforting responses from attachment figures, they may develop elevated levels of fear, anxiety, and distress that can persist into adulthood and impact later relationships.

Chapter 4

Changing Your Mindset

"The trick is not to get hooked on the highs and lows and mistake an activated attachment system for passion or love. Don't let emotional unavailability turn you on."
Amir Levine.

At its core, your mindset shapes your beliefs, values, and attitudes about yourself and the world you inhabit. It ultimately shapes how you perceive and experience the world. Depending on your mindset, you may either feel like life is happening to you, or it is happening for you. You may feel like you have complete control over your life or that your destiny is predetermined. You may believe strongly in personal growth, or conversely, you may be content living within the confines of your comfort zone.

People can often be described as "stuck in their ways", holding rigid beliefs that may be outdated or no longer serve them. Others may be seen as pessimistic, whereas some may be labeled optimists. These different labels are all indicative of the different types of mindsets people hold.

The good news is that it is possible to change your mindset. The ability to shift one's mindset is a key trait shared by successful people who have achieved their goals. Everyone is capable of changing their mindset, which can improve the quality of their life and even propel them towards their desired success. There are several ways to shift your mindset, and taking concrete steps toward cultivating a more positive and productive mindset can profoundly impact your personal and professional life.

Stop Gossiping

Have you ever found yourself venting about your partner's behavior to a friend or family member? While this may seem like a natural response to a frustrating situation, it is important to be mindful of the impact of negative talk on your relationships.

One reason why it's not ideal to talk about your partner negatively with others is that it can create a cycle of negative energy. As the saying goes, "What goes around comes around." If you engage in negative gossip about your partner, you are confirming to yourself that there is something fundamentally wrong in your relationship. By focusing on their flaws and making them the central topic of conversation, you are inadvertently amplifying their negative qualities in your mind.

It's important to remember that energy flows where focus goes. If all your energy is focused on the negative aspects of your relationship, it can be difficult to see the positive aspects. This can lead to further dissatisfaction and disappointment in your relationship, which can then be expressed through more negative talk.

Of course, it is understandable to want to share your frustrations with others from time to time. The key is to be mindful of how often you do it and to balance out the negative talk with positive talk. Rather than focusing solely on your partner's flaws, try to devote equal energy to discussing the positive aspects of your relationship. This can help shift your focus towards the positives and cultivate more positivity in your mind.

Adjusting to Your Partner's Mood

Let me illustrate a situation that you might find familiar. It's the weekend, and you've been excitedly looking forward to spending quality time with your partner. However, when the weekend arrives, your partner is in a bad mood due to a rough week and doesn't feel up for doing anything. In this scenario, it's easy to feel upset or annoyed.

But here's an alternative perspective: You can choose not to allow your partner's negative mood to affect your own emotions. This doesn't mean that you ignore or dismiss your partner's feelings; it simply means that you don't take on their mood as your own. By adopting this mindset, you can relieve the pressure on your relationship.

When you expect your partner to always be in a cheerful mood, it implies their role is to "make you happy." However, it's important to recognize that happiness is not solely your partner's responsibility—it is ultimately your own. This realization highlights the importance of taking ownership of your happiness.

By acknowledging that you have the power to cultivate happiness within yourself, you can relieve your partner of the burden of constantly ensuring your happiness. This shift in mindset allows you to approach your relationship from a place of understanding and support rather than harboring unrealistic expectations.

Be There for Yourself

Taking responsibility for your happiness is crucial not only in romantic relationships but in all aspects of life. We often have the desire for others to show up for us, meet our expectations, and make our lives easier. However, it is important to acknowledge that life is a journey of growth, and sometimes, people may not always do what we expect them to.

In the scenario mentioned earlier, where your partner doesn't want to participate in the activities you planned for the weekend, you have the opportunity to show up for yourself. Not showing up for yourself could involve feeling annoyed and spending the entire weekend on the sofa, indulging in popcorn and chocolate. However, showing up for yourself could look different. It might involve reaching out to friends to see what they're up to, enjoying a good book, or taking a peaceful solo walk.

You may wonder how this relates to the longevity of your relationship. When you allow yourself to stay sour and dwell in negative thoughts for the entire weekend, it can significantly impact your perception of your partner. Your thoughts about them are likely to be negative, and this can strain the relationship. On the other hand, when you show up for yourself and maintain a positive attitude, you can approach the situation with the understanding that everyone has bad days. By choosing to have a good time regardless of your partner's mood, you can move forward and nurture a healthier relationship.

Inner Wounds

We all carry inner wounds from our past experiences, whether from childhood or previous relationships. Unfortunately, these unresolved issues can often impact our current partnerships when we project our triggers onto our significant other.

It's common to fall into the belief that our partner shouldn't have behaved in a certain way or said certain things. However, it's essential to recognize that we have a choice in how we interpret and react to a situation. Our past experiences tend to condition us to think in a specific way, but it's crucial to challenge and explore these patterns. By doing so, we can let go of our emotional baggage and cultivate a more relaxed and open-minded attitude in our relationship.

Exploring and releasing our inner wounds not only allows us to heal and grow individually but also has a positive impact on our partnership. By addressing our baggage, we become more self-aware and less likely to blame our partner for triggering our old wounds. This newfound clarity and understanding create a healthier dynamic in the relationship.

When we let go of the limitations imposed by our past, we can approach our partners and situations with a fresh perspective. We understand they are not responsible for our past hurts, and we become more compassionate and empathetic towards them. This shift in mindset fosters better communication, trust, and overall harmony in the relationship.

Taking the time to work on ourselves and heal our inner wounds ultimately benefits not only our well-being but also the longevity and strength of our partnership. By embracing self-reflection and letting go of emotional baggage, we create space for growth, understanding, and a deeper connection with our significant other.

Don't Compare

Your thoughts have a significant impact on the relationship you have or desire to have. It may seem obvious, but it's worth emphasizing that creating the relationship of your dreams starts and continues with the thoughts you cultivate. Comparing your relationship to others, indulging in thoughts like "Why doesn't my partner do this like someone else's partner?" or even fantasizing about someone else can hinder the growth of your relationship.

When you find yourself thinking about others or making comparisons, you divert your attention and energy away from nurturing your relationship. As humans, we can only hold one thought at a time. So, by focusing on someone else's garden, you neglect the cultivation of your own. Instead of spending time and effort on your relationship, you're directing your energy towards something that isn't within your control.

If there are specific actions or behaviors that you desire from your partner but aren't currently receiving, it's important to take a proactive approach. Rather than dwelling on what your partner isn't doing, shift your mindset and water your garden. In other words, take actions that foster love and affection within your relationship. Show your partner acts of kindness and love that make them feel valued and cherished. By doing so, you redirect your focus towards love instead of dwelling on its absence. As a result, not only does your partner feel loved and appreciated, but you also cultivate a sense of love within yourself.

By continuously nourishing your relationship with positive thoughts and actions, you create an environment conducive to the growth and development of the relationship you desire. Remember, the grass may appear greener on the other side, but investing time and energy into your garden will yield a more fulfilling, authentic, and loving relationship.

Boundaries

In the past, I used to believe that it was only necessary to set boundaries for everyone except my romantic partner. However, I have come to realize just how mistaken I was. Boundaries are crucial for every person in our lives, especially our partners. Our significant others have a greater potential to unintentionally violate our boundaries simply because they are the closest to us and have more access to our personal space.

A key factor that played a role in my liberation was the realization that not establishing healthy boundaries is detrimental not only to myself but also to the other person involved. Looking back, I now recognize that I may have unknowingly crossed the emotional boundaries of others before I fully grasped the concept. Due to my lack of knowledge on how to safeguard myself through healthy boundaries, I allowed people to harm me emotionally. This lack of self-protection not only resulted in my suffering but also contributed to a negative impact on those around me.

Often, we only become aware of the need to establish boundaries when one of our boundaries is violated, which we may not have even known about. In such situations, we can choose to address the issue through open and honest communication or, depending on the circumstances, make a commitment to behave differently in the future. Boundaries primarily concern how we present ourselves and what we allow in our lives. Once we gain a deeper understanding of ourselves, we become better equipped to align our actions and behaviors with our true selves. This ultimately benefits our relationship, as when we remain true to ourselves, there is no need to place blame on others. I will speak more about boundaries later in the book.

Unconditional Love

It's essential to recognize that being in a relationship is a choice, and it's not always an easy one. However, we always have the option to leave if we are not happy or satisfied with where we are. I mention this because some of us tend to continually criticize our partners, even though we have no intention of ending the relationship.

Whether it's their eating habits or forgetfulness, when we constantly criticize our partners for their flaws, it indicates that we do not fully love and accept them as they are. While we may claim that we love them, our partners may not feel truly loved and accepted for who they are. This point is significant because we all yearn to be loved and accepted for our authentic selves. If we fail to fulfill our part by showing unconditional love and acceptance, tension in the relationship will likely build over time.

Cultivating Self-Compassion

Self-kindness and embracing our common humanity are two interconnected concepts that can greatly impact our well-being. They remind us of the following:

1. We are all human beings,

2. It is perfectly okay to be imperfect.

Instead of defining ourselves solely by our thoughts, feelings, and behaviors, we can practice self-compassion by giving ourselves the same leniency and understanding that we would extend to others.

For instance, if a friend neglects to answer your phone call out of laziness, you are unlikely to jump to the conclusion that they are a bad person. By permitting ourselves to be human, we can acknowledge and accept our flaws. This realization allows us to recognize that we are not alone in experiencing imperfections; it is a common aspect of the human condition.

Abigail grappled with deep-seated feelings of inadequacy and self-doubt. Seeking therapy, she confronted these issues head-on. Through self-reflection, she learned to challenge negative thoughts and treat herself with kindness.

Abigail embraced the idea of being a work in progress, understanding that mistakes are opportunities for growth. Instead of harsh self-criticism, she adopted a compassionate mindset. For instance, when she makes a mistake at work, Abigail reframes it as a chance to learn and improve.

By practicing self-compassion, Abigail found a balance between self-improvement and self-acceptance. She acknowledged her strengths and weaknesses without judgment, fostering inner peace.

An important aspect of self-compassion is treating ourselves with the same care and empathy we would offer to a friend in need. When a friend is feeling down, hurt, or upset, we may offer physical gestures of comfort, such as patting them on the back or holding their hand. Similarly, using gentle and forgiving language, including terms of endearment like "darling" or "sweetheart," can help cultivate self-kindness, even if it feels initially unfamiliar or awkward.

Becoming Self-Aware

If you find positive affirmations to be ineffective or unnatural, an alternative approach you can try is using "releasing statements." Releasing statements can be considered exercises in self-forgiveness and are closely related to the concept of detached non-judgment in mindfulness (Moore, 2019). Instead of engaging with negative thoughts, like "I'm such a horrible person for getting upset," you can turn it around and consciously "release" yourself from that negative feeling. For instance, you can say to yourself, "It's okay that I felt upset." This practice allows you to acknowledge and accept your emotions without attaching negative judgments to them.

Another important aspect of self-compassion is self-acceptance, which involves embracing your perceived weaknesses and character strengths. It's essential to avoid over-inflating or defining yourself solely based on these shortcomings. Instead, recognize that thoughts and feelings are simply behaviors and states, and they do not fully define who you are as a person.

Practicing mindfulness can be valuable in cultivating self-compassion. Mindfulness exercises help you stay present in the moment and can serve as a grounding technique. Not only is mindfulness one of the key components of self-compassion, but activities like yoga and deep breathing can be practiced anywhere and at any time, making them accessible tools for promoting self-care and self-acceptance.

Gaining Perspective

One way to cultivate self-kindness is by letting go of the need for outside validation. Often, when we berate ourselves for our choices, such as eating something indulgent, it is because we internalize societal pressures related to appearance and weight. By consciously deciding not to tie our happiness and self-worth to external influences, we can demonstrate self-compassion and positively impact our overall well-being. This act of self-kindness can have a ripple effect, allowing us to break free from the cycle of seeking validation from others and instead focus on nurturing our inner contentment.

Additionally, reaching out to others can be a valuable strategy for cultivating self-compassion. It may seem contradictory to the previous point, but this technique is about gaining perspective and placing our feelings within a larger context. When we engage in conversations with others and open up about our experiences, we often discover that we are not alone in experiencing pain or self-criticism. This realization reaffirms our sense of connectedness and helps us reframe our perceived problems within the bigger picture of shared human experiences. Moreover, reaching out creates an opportunity to build social support networks that play a crucial role in our overall well-being, providing understanding, empathy, and encouragement along our self-compassion journey.

Practical Exercises for Building Self-Love

Building self-love is a powerful practice that can significantly improve your overall well-being and relationships. Here are a few practical exercises you can incorporate into your daily routine to cultivate self-love:

Begin your day by stating positive affirmations about yourself. Repeat statements such as "I am worthy," "I am enough," and "I love and accept myself unconditionally." This helps rewire your thoughts towards self-compassion and strengthens self-love.

Whenever you find yourself being self-critical or experiencing difficult emotions, take a moment to pause. Acknowledge your feelings and remind yourself that it's okay to struggle. Then, offer yourself words of comfort and support, similar to what you would say to a close friend in a challenging situation.

Set aside a few minutes each day to write down things you appreciate and are grateful for about yourself. It could be your strengths, achievements, or qualities. Focusing on gratitude for your attributes can help cultivate self-love and appreciation.

Develop regular self-care practices that nurture your physical, emotional, and mental well-being. This could include activities like taking a hot bath, enjoying a cup of tea, practicing mindfulness or meditation, engaging in your favorite hobbies, or spending time in nature. Prioritize self-care as a way of showing love and care for yourself.

Set aside some time each week for self-reflection. Ask yourself how you're feeling, what you need in the moment, and any areas where you need to offer yourself more compassion. Listen to your intuition and be kind and gentle with yourself.

Surround yourself with people who support and uplift you. Seek out positive role models, inspiring books, podcasts, or online communities that promote self-love and personal growth.

Strategies for Overcoming Self-Critical Thoughts

Here are some strategies for overcoming self-critical thoughts:

Start by becoming aware of your self-critical thoughts. When you notice negative self-talk, challenge it by asking yourself if it's rooted in reality or a distorted perception. Look for evidence that supports or contradicts the negative thoughts and try to reframe them in a more realistic and compassionate light.

Pay attention to when and why self-critical thoughts appear. Is there a specific trigger or situation that tends to activate them? By understanding the patterns and underlying causes, you can better address and challenge these thoughts. Mindfulness practices, such as meditation or journaling, can help cultivate self-awareness and reduce self-critical thinking.

Instead of viewing mistakes as personal failures, reframe them as valuable learning experiences. Embrace the opportunity to grow, develop new skills, and gain wisdom from your experiences. Remember that nobody is perfect, and growth comes from embracing and learning from failures.

Create a list of your achievements and review it regularly. Celebrate even the small victories and acts of self-improvement. You can treat yourself to some pizza or ice cream. With time, this practice can help rewire your brain to focus on your strengths and foster self-appreciation rather than self-criticism.

Reframing Negative Thought Patterns

The way we think, feel, and behave are intricately connected and continuously impact each other. Sometimes, however, we develop patterns of thoughts or behaviors that are unhelpful and detrimental to our well-being. This can create a vicious cycle where these negative patterns influence our emotions, which then further impact our thoughts and behaviors.

Unfortunately, many of us are unaware that we have the power to influence and improve this process, ultimately enhancing our mental health. One effective method is to challenge and replace these unhelpful thoughts. By doing so, we can effectively address stress and anxiety, improve our sleep patterns, and significantly elevate our overall mood. This, in turn, can have a transformative effect on our mental health and overall sense of well-being.

To accomplish this, it is essential to learn how to take a step back and examine our thoughts critically. By questioning the evidence that supports these negative thoughts, we can gradually shift them towards more positive and constructive ones. With practice and dedication, it is possible to reshape our thought patterns and cultivate a more optimistic and resilient mindset. This shift in thinking can have a profound and lasting impact on our mental health, leading to improved well-being and a more fulfilling life.

Here are a few examples:

Example 1:

- **Negative Thought:** "I made a mistake. I'm so stupid."

- **Reframed Thought:** "Making mistakes is part of being human. This mistake is an opportunity for me to learn and grow. I can take this experience as a chance to improve my skills and be more careful in the future."

Example 2:

- **Negative Thought:** "I failed my exam. I'm a complete failure."

- **Reframed Thought:** "Failing an exam doesn't define my worth. It's an indication that I need to adjust my studying approach or seek help if necessary. This setback is an opportunity for me to reflect, regroup, and approach future exams more effectively."

Example 3:

- **Negative Thought:** "I was rejected when I asked someone out. I'm unlovable."

- **Reframed Thought:** "Rejection is a normal part of life, and it doesn't reflect my worth as a person. This experience means that I had the courage to take a chance, and it's simply an opportunity to find someone who appreciates and reciprocates my feelings."

When reframing negative thoughts, you can ask yourself questions like:

- Is this thought based on factual evidence, or is it a distortion?

- How would I respond if a friend or loved one had the same experience or thought?

- How can I reframe this thought in a more compassionate and realistic way?

- What can I learn from this situation? What opportunities for growth does it present?

- How can I view this experience from a different perspective or with greater understanding?

You can certainly add these reframed thoughts and the questions you ask yourself to your journal. Writing down negative thoughts and challenging them with reframed thoughts and questions can help you gain clarity, develop self-awareness, and foster a more positive and compassionate mindset.

Steps and Strategies

It is often the case that we are unaware when we engage in unhelpful thinking patterns. This can make it hard to recognize these thoughts in the first place. However, we can learn to identify what sort of thoughts are unhelpful in making the spotting process easier.

Unhelpful thoughts come in different forms, such as always expecting the worst from any situation, only focusing on the negative sides of a situation, seeing things as either good or bad with nothing in between, and considering oneself the sole cause behind unfortunate events.

Being aware of these categories of negative thoughts is essential, and if you have an unhelpful thought throughout your day, you can identify which category it belongs to. Although it may seem difficult to tune into these thoughts initially, being familiar with the types of unhelpful thoughts can help you recognize and reduce the frequency of them. With practice, this skill of reflecting on your thoughts will become more natural, and you will be able to spot them instantly.

Once you have identified an unhelpful thought, the next step is to assess it fully. You can do this by taking a step back and reviewing the situation. For instance, you may be worried about failing a significant task at work and believing everyone calls you a failure for it.

Rather than accepting this thought, take a quantifiable amount of time to check it. Ask yourself some questions surrounding the thought, such as how likely the outcome of the task is, whether there is good proof to support the thought, whether there are other possibilities, whether there are alternative ways to approach the situation, and what you say to a friend suffering from similar thoughts.

When you have successfully identified and examined your negative thoughts, strive to reframe them to more positive or neutral ones. Reflect on your questions when assessing the thought and see how you can approach the situation differently.

If you can't turn the negative thought into a positive one, don't worry. This process isn't about having right or wrong answers. It is about developing flexibility in your thinking patterns and gaining control over your thoughts. Learning to distinguish helpful and unhelpful thoughts, as well as finding a new perspective, can break the cycle of negative thoughts and bring about a fresh outlook, often making the situation less intense than you initially thought. I will discuss this further later in the book.

Additional Tips to Change Unhelpful Thinking

Negative thinking patterns can have a significant impact on our well-being and overall mindset. It is important to recognize these patterns in order to replace them with more helpful and positive thoughts. Some commonly observed negative thinking patterns include:

- **Black and white thinking:** This is when we see things as either completely right or completely wrong, with no room for shades of gray or alternative perspectives. It limits our ability to see different possibilities and can lead to extreme judgments.

- **Personalizing:** In this thinking pattern, we tend to take personal responsibility for everything that goes wrong, disregarding external factors or circumstances that may have contributed to the outcome. This can be self-blaming and put unnecessary pressure on ourselves.

- **Filter thinking:** This occurs when we selectively focus only on the negative aspects of a situation or person, ignoring any positive aspects. It can create a distorted perception and prevent us from seeing the whole picture.

- **Catastrophizing:** This involves constantly imagining and assuming the worst-case scenarios, even when there is little evidence to support such catastrophic outcomes. It often leads to unnecessary anxiety and stress.

Recognizing these negative thinking patterns is the first step towards replacing them with more helpful thoughts. Mindfulness practices, such as meditation, can assist in redirecting our focus to the present moment and distancing ourselves from depressive thoughts and emotions. By detaching ourselves, we can view our negative thoughts objectively and challenge them more easily.

Keeping a thought diary is another effective technique to interrupt negative thoughts. By writing down our negative thinking styles, we gain a better understanding of their impact on our emotional reactions. This self-reflection helps us identify patterns and provides an opportunity for us to reframe our thoughts more positively and realistically.

Focusing on gratitude is also a powerful tool to counteract negative thinking. Even during challenging times, make an effort to think about three things you are grateful for each day, even if they are small. Shifting our attention to what we appreciate helps cultivate a more positive mindset.

However, if negative thoughts persist or become overwhelming, seeking professional help from a therapist is highly recommended. While friends and family can provide support and perspective, a mental health professional can offer specialized guidance and provide additional tools and strategies to effectively change our thinking patterns. It is essential to prioritize our mental well-being and seek appropriate support when needed.

Overcoming Self-Doubt

Self-doubt can arise from various sources, such as past negative experiences or anxious attachment style issues. Individuals with insecure attachment styles may have been subjected to criticism, which can later contribute to self-doubt. Such individuals may find it challenging to trust their abilities or judgment. Furthermore, negative experiences in the past, such as being discouraged or told that they are not good enough, can create a lasting impact on their self-worth and increase self-doubt.

In addition to personal experiences, societal pressure to achieve can be another source of self-doubt. The constant pressure to be successful and meet unreasonable standards can lead to fears of failure and inadequacy. Instead of motivating individuals, this pressure can create additional insecurities and amplify self-doubt.

If left unaddressed, self-doubt can have significant consequences. It can lead to anxiety, depression, procrastination, emotional instability, low self-esteem, and difficulty making decisions. These negative effects can be detrimental to an individual's overall well-being and prevent them from reaching their full potential.

Therefore, recognizing and addressing self-doubt is crucial for promoting emotional and mental health. Seeking support from a therapist, adopting self-care strategies, and challenging negative thoughts are effective methods of reducing self-doubt. By developing self-compassion and practicing positivity and mindfulness, individuals can improve their self-confidence and reduce self-doubt. Taking action to address self-doubt can help individuals overcome obstacles and achieve their goals.

Start by becoming aware of the self-doubting thoughts that arise in your mind. Pay attention to the negative statements you tell yourself and challenge them by asking for evidence that supports or contradicts those thoughts. Replace self-doubt with more compassionate and realistic self-talk. For example, if you catch yourself thinking, "I can't do this," remind yourself of times when you have overcome challenges in the past and reframe the thought to "I may face challenges, but I am capable and have what it takes to succeed."

Surround yourself with positive and supportive people who believe in your abilities. Seek out friends, mentors, or a supportive community who can offer encouragement and provide constructive feedback. Share your goals and aspirations with them, and allow their belief in you to strengthen your self-belief.

Also, break down your goals into smaller, achievable steps. By setting realistic goals and taking action, you build momentum and gain confidence in your abilities. Celebrate each small success along the way, reinforcing your belief in yourself and your capabilities. It would help if you also used visualization techniques to imagine yourself successfully accomplishing your goals. Visualizing positive outcomes can help rewire your brain and build confidence in your abilities. Practice visualizing yourself confidently overcoming challenges, and achieving the things you desire.

Overcoming self-doubt is an ongoing process. Be patient with yourself and commit to these exercises regularly. With persistence and practice, you can gradually build self-belief and overcome self-doubt.

Imposter Syndrome

Imposter syndrome is a psychological phenomenon that often accompanies self-doubt. It refers to the overwhelming feeling of being a fraud or an imposter despite evidence of achievements and accomplishments. Imposter syndrome is commonly experienced, particularly among women and minority groups, who may face additional societal pressure and stereotypes ("Rising above the Imposter Syndrome Trap on Women & Minorities," n.d.).

The impact of imposter syndrome is profound. It can hinder individuals from taking risks, pursuing new opportunities, or fully showcasing their abilities. The fear of being exposed as inadequate or unworthy can prevent individuals from putting themselves out there in a meaningful way. Even though they have accomplished great things, imposter syndrome causes them to doubt their qualifications, performance, and overall competence. This self-doubt can manifest in various areas of life, including work, relationships, friendships, parenting, and other activities.

The negative effect of self-doubt and imposter syndrome on self-esteem cannot be underestimated. Constantly questioning one's abilities and feeling like an imposter diminishes a person's confidence and belief in their worth. It can lead to feelings of inadequacy, anxiety, and fear of failure.

Fortunately, there are strategies that can help combat self-doubt and imposter syndrome and cultivate self-confidence. One powerful approach is to reframe negative thoughts and challenge the imposter syndrome narrative. Recognizing and acknowledging achievements, skills, and successes can help rewire the belief that one is a fraud. It is important to celebrate and internalize accomplishments, giving oneself credit for the hard work and effort put into achieving those goals.

Building a support network of trusted individuals who provide encouragement and validation can also be instrumental in combating self-doubt. Surrounding oneself with people who believe in their abilities and provide constructive feedback can help counteract feelings of being an imposter. Seeking mentorship and guidance from successful individuals who have faced similar challenges can provide inspiration and guidance.

Practicing self-care and self-compassion is another key component of overcoming self-doubt. Taking time for personal well-being, engaging in activities that bring joy and fulfillment, and acknowledging one's strengths and value is crucial in building self-confidence and combating imposter syndrome.

It is important to remember that self-doubt and imposter syndrome are common experiences, and many successful individuals have dealt with them. Seeking professional help from a therapist or counselor can provide further guidance and support in navigating these feelings and developing strategies to overcome self-doubt.

Chapter Summary

- Mindset shapes beliefs, values, and attitudes about oneself and the world.

- Different mindsets may result in different perceptions of life.

- People can change their mindset to improve their quality of life and achieve success.

- Being able to shift one's mindset is a key trait of successful people.

- Cultivating a positive and productive mindset can have a profound impact on personal and professional life.

Chapter 5

Communication and Connection

"Communication is the solvent of all problems and is the foundation for personal development."
Peter Shepherd.

Effective communication is vital for positive social interaction and overcoming anxious attachment. However, it can be challenging to have a healthy conversation and avoid over-communicating. This is especially important in romantic relationships.

A common communication model involves a sender, a receiver, and a message that is encoded by the sender and decoded by the receiver. This model also includes feedback from the receiver and any noise that could disrupt the communication process.

Encoding refers to the sender transforming their thoughts into communicable messages while the receiver interprets the message they receive, both verbally and nonverbally. However, this process is not as straightforward as it seems, as some personal filters and biases can influence how the message is decoded.

In addition, messages are not purely factual information. According to Friedemann Schulz von Thun's Four-Sides model of communication, every message has four facets: the factual aspect, self-revelation, the relationship aspect, and an appeal (Domendos, 2021). The emphasis placed on each facet can vary, and the intended meaning may differ from the perceived meaning. For example, a wife saying "the sugar jar is empty" may be less about the fact itself and more of a hint for her husband to refill the jar.

Furthermore, as receivers, we often have one facet that we are more attuned to, such as focusing on the factual aspect, the relationship aspect, self-revelation, or the appeal. This can further complicate communication, as misinterpretations can occur when the emphasis placed on each facet varies between the sender and receiver.

This type of breakdown in communication can lead to misunderstandings and conflicts. It is essential to recognize that what we hear may not accurately reflect what the other person intended to convey. It is important to be aware of our own biases and tendencies in order to engage in healthy communication.

To improve communication, it is crucial to understand and consider all four facets of the message. For instance, when feeling questioned or misunderstood, it can be helpful to go back to the original statement and assess the various aspects. By focusing on factual information and using questions to clarify understanding, we can better grasp the intended message and avoid unnecessary conflicts or misunderstandings.

Relationships With No Communication

If there is a lack of communication in a relationship, it is possible that both parties are not truly listening to each other. Instead, they may be more focused on proving themselves right or engaging in simultaneous tasks that distract from active listening.

Several common listening mistakes can hinder effective communication:

- Daydreaming or allowing thoughts to wander while the other person is speaking, even if it's something as mundane as thinking about a grocery list.

- Preparing a response in your mind instead of fully engaging with what the other person is saying.

- Judging or critiquing the other person's words instead of trying to understand their perspective.

- Listening with a specific goal or desired outcome in mind can limit the ability to truly hear and comprehend the other person.

However, active listening encompasses much more than simply refraining from talking. It is an art that requires a genuine interest in the other person and a curiosity rather than a preoccupied mindset. Active listening involves:

- Demonstrating nonverbal involvement to show attention, such as making eye contact and nodding.

- Focusing on the person in front of you rather than your thoughts.

- Avoiding judgment and creating a safe space for open expression.

- Being comfortable with moments of silence can allow for deeper understanding and reflection.

One practical exercise to revive communication in a relationship is called "The Listening Exercise." Set aside a specific time for both partners to participate in this exercise, free from distractions. Decide who will go first and who will be the listener. The speaker will have 10-15 minutes to talk about their thoughts, feelings, and concerns without interruption from the listener (Freed, 2023).

The listener's role is listening actively without offering advice, judgment, or solution. After the speaker has finished, the listener will summarize what they heard, focusing on the speaker's emotions and main points. When the listener has summarized, the roles will be reversed, and the other partner will have their turn to speak while the first partner listens.

Repeat this exercise regularly, for example, every weekend, allowing both partners equal time to speak and be heard. This exercise helps to improve communication by providing a safe space for each partner to express themselves fully while the other partner practices active listening. It promotes understanding, empathy, and a deeper connection between partners.

Better Communication

When it comes to addressing a situation like your date arriving late, it's important to communicate your observations without adding labels or interpretations. Instead of assuming that their lateness reflects a lack of interest or prioritization, stick to the facts. Simply acknowledge, "I noticed you were late for our date." This statement highlights your observation without any evaluation or judgment.

Effective communication involves more than just sharing observations; it also requires expressing emotions. When emotions are left unexpressed, they can build up and eventually lead to arguments, misunderstandings, and resentment. Therefore, it is important to take the time to understand and communicate your feelings.

Understanding your emotions is a crucial first step in expressing them effectively. Take the time to reflect on what you are feeling and why you feel that way. Identify the specific emotions you are experiencing, whether it's annoyance, frustration, sadness, or any other feeling. This self-awareness will help you articulate your emotions more clearly.

Once you have identified your emotions, express them to your partner in a non-judgmental manner. Avoid attacking or blaming your partner, as this can escalate the situation. Instead, use "I" statements to take ownership of your emotions and communicate how you are feeling. For example, instead of saying, "You always make me angry," you could say, "I am feeling annoyed right now."

When expressing your emotions, try to provide context and explain why you feel the way you do. Help your partner understand the impact their actions or words have had on you. For instance, you could say, "I am bothered by this because it makes me wonder whether you are looking forward to spending time with me."

By openly sharing your emotions, you provide your partner with insight into your emotional state and foster a better understanding of your perspective. This can lead to more empathetic and constructive communication. It allows both you and your partner to have a deeper connection and work towards resolving any issues or conflicts that may arise.

Furthermore, it's essential to understand and communicate your needs. Expressing your needs allows your partner to evaluate if they can fulfill them while also giving them an opportunity to prioritize your relationship. This also helps alleviate anxious attachment fears. For example, you might say, "I would like to be treated with consideration, and I want to feel important to you." By articulating your needs, you establish a clear framework for what you expect from the relationship.

The final step is to make a direct request. Clearly communicate what your partner needs to do in order for your needs to be met. In this case, you could say something like, "That is why I ask you to arrive at the agreed-upon time." By making a specific request, you outline the concrete action that would address your needs and improve the situation

Active Listening Techniques

Maintaining appropriate eye contact is crucial in face-to-face conversations. However, it's important to find a balance, as excessive eye contact can be intimidating. To adapt to the situation, consider breaking eye contact every five seconds or so. Additionally, to show active listening, focus on one eye for five seconds, switch to the other eye for another five seconds, and then shift your gaze towards their mouth. If you need to look away, it's better to look to the side or up rather than down, as looking downwards can indicate disinterest and a desire to end the conversation. Do this as many times as you want. The more you do it, the better it helps improve your techniques.

In addition to actively listening and engaging in verbal communication, it is important to pay attention to your posture and be aware of non-verbal cues during conversations. Posture plays a significant role in conveying openness and attentiveness.

To create an open posture, make sure to avoid crossing your arms or legs, as this can give off a closed-off or defensive vibe. Instead, keep your arms relaxed at your sides or place them comfortably on your lap. Similarly, avoid slouching or leaning back too far, as this may indicate disinterest. Instead, aim to sit upright or lean slightly forward or sideways, as this demonstrates that you are actively listening and engaged in the conversation.

Non-verbal cues such as a slight tilt of your head or resting your head on your hand can also indicate attentiveness. These cues signal to the speaker that you are interested in what they have to say and that you are actively processing their words.

Developing a habit of maintaining an open posture can greatly enhance your communication skills. By consistently practicing open body language, it will become more natural and effortless for you to maintain an open and engaged posture during conversations.

Effective listening involves not only paying attention to verbal communication but also being attentive to non-verbal cues. Facial expressions, tone of voice, and gestures can provide valuable information about a person's emotions and thoughts.

Observing the other person's body language can give you insight into their level of engagement and comfort. Are they smiling and maintaining eye contact, indicating that they are responsive and interested, or are they crossing their arms defensively, suggesting they may be guarded or disengaged? Paying attention to these cues allows you to better understand the underlying emotions and thoughts behind their words.

Even during phone conversations where visual cues are absent, it is essential to be mindful of the tone of the person's voice. The tone can convey subtle nuances and emotions that may not be explicitly expressed in their words. Listen for changes in pitch, volume, and pacing, as these can provide insights into their emotional state or attitude.

Avoid jumping in and interrupting the other person. Interrupting can be frustrating for them and gives the impression that you consider your thoughts or time more important. If you tend to be a quick thinker or speaker, make a conscious effort to slow down and allow the other person to express themselves fully. Remember, it's not necessary to jump in immediately during pauses or moments of silence.

One practical exercise to improve active listening skills is "Reflective Listening." Choose a topic or scenario to practice active listening. One partner will be the speaker, and the other will be the listener. The speaker will share their thoughts, feelings, or experiences about the chosen topic for two to three minutes. The listener's role is to actively listen and refrain from interrupting or responding verbally (UNSW Teaching Staff Gateway, n.d.).

After the speaker has finished speaking, the listener will then reflect on what they heard, using phrases such as, "It sounds like you're saying..." or "I hear you saying..." The speaker will confirm whether the reflection is accurate or provide clarification.

Switch roles, where the speaker becomes the listener and vice versa. Repeat the exercise with different topics or scenarios to continue practicing active listening. This exercise helps improve active listening by encouraging individuals to focus on what the speaker is saying without immediately offering their thoughts or opinions. It also allows the listener to demonstrate understanding and empathy by reflecting on what they heard, which can enhance effective communication and foster deeper connections in relationships.

Demonstrate active listening through non-verbal cues. Nod your head, smile, and make small verbal affirmations like "yes" and "uh huh" to show that you're engaged and encourage the speaker to continue. Avoid looking at your watch, fidgeting, or playing with your hair or fingernails, as these behaviors can be distracting and indicate disinterest.

Resist the urge to impose your opinions or solutions. Instead, provide a listening and supportive ear. Listening attentively can be much more rewarding for the other person than receiving unsolicited advice. For example, when a loved one is facing health problems, they often want to express their feelings and talk about their experiences rather than receiving an abundance of advice on what they should do. In other areas of life, most individuals prefer to come to their solutions. If you feel compelled to share your ideas, ask first if they would like to hear them. For instance, say something like, "Would you like to hear my suggestions?"

Asking relevant questions can demonstrate that you've been actively listening and help clarify information. If you're unsure whether you've understood something correctly, wait until the speaker pauses and then ask for clarification, such as saying, "Did you mean that x..." or "I'm not sure if I understood what you were saying about..."

Incorporating open-ended questions, when appropriate, can also be beneficial. These questions, like "How did that make you feel?" or "What did you do next?" can encourage the person to share more about their experiences and thoughts.

Expressing Your Needs and Setting Boundaries

Effective communication is crucial when it comes to expressing your needs to others, especially loved ones. Rushed conversations, unclear language, and vague requests can make it difficult for others to understand and respect your boundaries.

One important factor to consider is timing. It is best to establish boundaries with your partner when both of you are relaxed and able to focus on
the conversation. If you find yourselves in the midst of an argument, it may
be beneficial to take a step back and revisit the topic once both of you have
calmed down.

Being prepared can also contribute to effective communication. If you feel
nervous about discussing your needs, it may be helpful to write down your
points before the conversation. This way, you can articulate your needs
clearly and concisely.

Let's look at the story of Mike and Emily. They had been together for a few
years and deeply loved each other. However, over time, they started feeling
overwhelmed and noticed a decline in their well-being.

Emily, a hardworking woman, felt drained and exhausted at the end of
each day. Mike, on the other hand, struggled with anxiety and constantly worried about the future. They both realized that they needed to set
boundaries in their relationship to maintain balance and preserve their
mental and emotional health.

One evening, after a particularly stressful day, Emily gathered her courage
and approached Mike to discuss their boundaries. She expressed her need
for some personal time after work to decompress and engage in activities
that rejuvenate her. Emily explained that this didn't mean she loved Mike
any less; she just needed space to recharge and care for herself.

Initially taken aback, Mike slowly started to understand and appreciate
Emily's perspective. He realized that her well-being was crucial for the
overall health of their relationship. Inspired by Emily's courage, he also
shared his need for open communication and reassurance when his anxiety
spiked, without feeling judged or overwhelmed.

They agreed to support each other in asserting and respecting these boundaries. Emily began setting aside time in the evenings for self-care, whether reading, taking walks, or enjoying her hobbies. Mike, in turn, initiated open conversations with Emily whenever he felt overwhelmed, allowing them to address his anxiety together.

As both partners started prioritizing their needs and respecting each other's boundaries, their relationship flourished. They felt more connected, understood, and balanced. By establishing boundaries, they protected their mental and emotional well-being and nurtured a healthier, more fulfilling relationship.

From that point forward, Mike and Emily continued to communicate openly about their boundaries, adapting as needed, and their relationship grew stronger with each passing day. They had learned the valuable lesson that setting and respecting boundaries was a sign of love and respect not only for themselves but also for their partner.

When communicating your boundaries, try to use "I" statements to express how you feel. Avoid using "you" statements, as they can come across as accusing or confrontational. For example, instead of saying, "You never help around the house," you could say, "I feel overwhelmed with the amount of work I have to do when you're away." Expressing your emotions in a non-confrontational manner can lay the groundwork for establishing boundaries in a relationship.

Clarity is key when expressing your needs. While a vague request may get the message across, it is better to be as specific as possible to avoid confusion. For instance, instead of saying, "I'd like more personal space," you could say, "I feel disrespected and uncomfortable when you come into my room without knocking. Please knock before entering." Using a calm but firm tone conveys that you are serious about your boundaries while still being respectful.

It is important to address any feedback or questions your partner may have about your boundary. While you are not obligated to justify your needs or explain yourself, doing so can help the other person understand where you are coming from. You may even ask follow-up questions to ensure your message is effectively conveyed.

In romantic relationships, it is especially important to ask your partner how they feel about a request instead of assuming their reaction. Ask if they find your request unfair or unusual. Inquire whether it conflicts with their own needs or wants. Each person in the relationship has their thoughts and feelings, and it is each individual's responsibility to communicate them clearly in order to be understood.

Remember that you are not responsible for how the other person reacts to your boundary. While it is natural to care about the other person's feelings and reactions, you should not disregard your own needs. For example, if the other person feels upset or disagrees with your request for more "me time," it is important to remind yourself why you are setting this boundary in the first place. You want some time alone to pursue your hobbies and avoid feeling emotionally overwhelmed. You should not feel guilty or selfish for prioritizing your own needs in this situation.

Enforcing Boundaries

It is important to acknowledge that not everyone in your life will always respect your boundaries. In some cases, a partner may accidentally cross a boundary, while difficult family members may intentionally do so.

When someone crosses a boundary, it can be helpful to restate your needs. It is possible that the other person didn't fully understand your original request or may have forgotten it. In this situation, it is important to remain calm, firm, and clear about what you need. Clearly articulate the boundary that was crossed and express how it made you feel. For example, you might say, "I feel disrespected when you talk over me. It is important to me that we have equal opportunity to express ourselves in our conversations."

Establishing clear and reasonable consequences for crossing a boundary can also be effective. For example, if someone has a habit of talking over you, you might communicate a consequence by saying, "If you talk over me again, I will have to end the conversation." This communicates the seriousness of the issue and demonstrates that there will be consequences for crossing the boundary.

However, it is important to only state the consequences you are willing to enforce. If you are not willing to follow through on a consequence, the other person may feel empowered to continue crossing your boundaries in the future. For instance, if you tell your partner that you will take a break from the relationship if they keep lying to you, it is crucial to actually follow through on that consequence if the boundary continues to be crossed. This reinforces the importance of setting boundaries and maintaining their integrity.

Setting and enforcing consequences can be challenging, especially in close relationships. However, doing so is essential for establishing and maintaining healthy boundaries. By consistently reinforcing your boundaries and the consequences for crossing them, you send a clear message that your needs must be respected.

Responding When Others Set Boundaries

It is important to remember that boundaries are not only established by you but by others in your life as well. When someone sets a boundary, it may trigger negative emotions such as shame or frustration. However, it is essential to approach these conversations with an open mind and willingness to understand.

When faced with boundaries that trigger negative emotions, taking the time to breathe and actively listen can be helpful. Deep breathing can help calm your nervous system's response, enabling you to be more receptive to the information being shared.

It is important to remember that the person setting the boundary knows what is best for themselves. While you may have your thoughts and preferences, expressing your needs in order to find a compromise that works for both parties is crucial.

Respecting boundaries means giving your partner the space to voice their needs without jumping to conclusions or making assumptions. Each person processes and experiences emotions differently, so it is important to allow them the opportunity to express themselves without judgment or interruption.

Apologizing when necessary is crucial in respecting boundaries. If you inadvertently overstep a boundary, it is important to be humble and apologize for your mistake. Additionally, if there is any confusion, ask for clarity to ensure you fully understand the boundary and how to respect it moving forward.

By accepting and acknowledging the boundaries set by others, you can improve your connections and relationships with those around you. Effective boundaries create a sense of empowerment for both parties involved and contribute to a healthier and more fulfilling relationship overall.

Guidelines and Examples for Assertive Communication

When practicing assertive communication, it is important to use "I" statements to express your thoughts and feelings. This helps take ownership of your perspective and avoids blaming or accusing the other person. By saying "I feel" or "I need," you are clearly conveying your own experiences and requirements.

In addition, it is crucial to be clear and specific when communicating your needs, thoughts, or concerns. Avoid using vague or ambiguous statements that can lead to misunderstandings. Instead, be explicit about what you want or expect. This allows the other person to better understand your request or concern and respond accordingly.

Projecting confidence and assertiveness through your body language is also key. This includes standing tall, maintaining eye contact, and speaking in a clear and firm voice. Avoid defensive postures like crossing your arms or avoiding eye contact, as these may convey a lack of confidence. By displaying assertive body language, you are more likely to be taken seriously and have your message heard.

Practicing active listening is another important aspect of assertive communication. This involves giving complete attention to the speaker and showing that you understand by summarizing or paraphrasing what they have said. Active listening demonstrates respect and helps prevent misunderstandings or misinterpretations.

Keeping a calm and composed demeanor throughout the conversation is essential, even if it becomes emotional or intense. Take deep breaths and pause when necessary to collect your thoughts. Respond thoughtfully rather than reacting impulsively. Remaining calm allows for a more constructive and productive dialogue.

Here are some examples of assertive communication:

- **Requesting a change:** Instead of blaming or demanding, clearly state your needs and expectations. For example, "I need you to complete the report by tomorrow as agreed upon so we can meet the deadline and avoid any delays."

- **Expressing boundaries:** It is important to assert your boundaries and communicate what makes you comfortable. For instance, "I am not comfortable sharing personal information at work. I prefer to keep my personal life separate from my professional life."

- **Giving feedback:** Provide constructive feedback by acknowledging effort and suggesting improvements. For example, "I appreciate your effort on this project, but I think there are areas that could be improved. Can we discuss potential solutions to enhance the quality?"

- **Saying no:** It is okay to say no when you are overwhelmed or unable to take on additional tasks. Be clear and assertive in expressing your limitations. For instance, "I have a lot on my plate at the moment, and I won't be able to take on any additional tasks right now. I encourage you to look for alternative resources."

- **Disagreeing respectfully:** When you have a different perspective, it is important to express it respectfully. You can say, "I see your point of view, but I have a different perspective on this matter. Can we explore both sides and find a middle ground?"

Navigating Conflict

Falling in love is undoubtedly a beautiful experience filled with excitement, joy, and an almost euphoric feeling. However, as time goes by, the initial romantic bliss may fade, and you may find yourself facing challenging issues in your relationship. Misunderstandings, heated arguments, placing blame, or growing apart due to differences can all lead to a strained relationship. To prevent this from happening and ensure a healthy, lasting relationship, it is important to learn effective conflict resolution skills. Here are some tips to help you navigate through conflicts and positively resolve them.

Express Yourself

There might be times when you choose to hold back your grievances with your partner, thinking that you will address them later. However, if left unresolved, these unspoken grievances can accumulate and gain emotional momentum, leading to a destructive outcome, much like a tornado. It is crucial for the health of your relationship that both you and your partner openly and directly express your concerns in a firm, honest, and compassionate manner.

To initiate these discussions, it is important to start by showing consideration for your partner's feelings. You can say something like, "I deeply care about our relationship," or "I know you don't intend to upset me."

This will help create a foundation for open and respectful communication. Next, clearly describe the behavior or action that is bothering you, providing specific details. It is important to express the feelings that arise within you, whether it be anger, hurt, irritation, frustration, or confusion. By sharing these emotions, you allow your partner to understand the impact of their actions on you.

After expressing your concerns, it is essential to ask for a specific change you would like to see. For example, you could say, "I would prefer it if you spoke to me in a calm and gentle tone," or "I would appreciate it if you could wait until I finish speaking before responding." By clearly stating your desired change, you give your partner a tangible action they can work on.

Finally, it is important to ask for an agreement at the end of your request. This gives your partner the opportunity to respond and discuss whether they are willing to make the change you have asked for. For instance, you can ask, "Are you willing to agree to this request?" By seeking agreement, you promote a sense of teamwork and collaboration in finding a resolution.

Take a moment to reflect on how effectively you express yourself in various aspects of your life. Consider your communication skills, ability to share your thoughts and feelings, and how comfortable you are expressing yourself. Rate yourself on a scale of 1-5, with 1 being low and 5 being high, for each statement below:

- I am able to convey my opinions and ideas clearly and confidently.

- I am at ease when it comes to expressing my emotions and vulnerability to others.

- I pay close attention when others speak and show empathy and understanding.

- I am able to communicate my needs and boundaries assertively without being aggressive.

- I am open to constructive feedback and willing to engage in productive conversations.

- I adjust my communication style depending on the situation and the needs of others.

- I actively seek opportunities to improve my communication skills through learning and practice.

- I am mindful of nonverbal communication cues and use them to my advantage.

- I am able to handle conflicts and disagreements in a respectful and positive way.

- I recognize my strengths and areas in which I need to improve in terms of communication.

Once you have rated yourself for each statement, take a moment to reflect on your answers. Identify areas where you feel strong and confident in expressing yourself and where you could benefit from growth or improvement. Consider setting specific goals or actions to enhance your ability to express yourself effectively in those areas.

This self-assessment is a tool for self-reflection and can help guide personal development. It is not meant to be an evaluation or judgment but rather an opportunity to understand yourself better and improve your communication skills.

Avoid the Blame Game

In relationships, it is common to feel tempted to blame our partners for various problems that arise. Whether it is something they said, did, or didn't do, the reasons for assigning blame can seem endless. However, engaging in the blame game rarely leads to positive outcomes. When one person is blamed, they often feel attacked, which triggers a defensive response rather than addressing the actual issue at hand. For example, if a partner says, "You're crazy for thinking that!" in response to a fear of infidelity, the blame instantly shifts away from the real issue. The other partner will likely react defensively, saying, "I'm crazy? You're the one who's crazy!"

Instead of engaging in the blame game, it is important to use "I feel" statements to handle conflicts in a relationship. This approach keeps the focus on the specific issue and avoids attacking the other person. By using "I feel" statements, you communicate your emotions and concerns without putting your partner down. This approach encourages better communication and leads to more constructive results.

By avoiding blame and focusing on expressing your feelings, you create a safe space for open dialogue and problem-solving. It also recognizes and honors the emotions of your partner, fostering a sense of empathy and understanding. Remember, conflicts are an opportunity for growth and strengthening your relationship when handled with care and respect.

One Argument at a Time

It is common for an argument to start with a specific topic and then unexpectedly spiral into various other related issues. This can be compared to a car losing control on black ice during winter. In order to maintain a healthy and productive argument, it is important to be aware of this tendency and stay focused on one topic at a time.

Let's look at a short story. Sarah and John had been together for several years. They were generally happy and loved each other deeply. However, like any couple, they occasionally had disagreements.

One day, Sarah came home from work feeling exhausted and stressed. She noticed that John had left his dirty clothes on the bedroom floor. Though minor, it irritated her because they had previously discussed the importance of tidiness in their home. Without thinking much, Sarah confronted John about the clothes and asked him to pick them up. Preoccupied with a project at work, John responded with a sigh and said he'd do it later.

Feeling unheard, Sarah's frustration grew. She couldn't understand why John wouldn't simply pick up after himself. The conversation quickly escalated into an argument as Sarah accused John of not caring about their home or her feelings. In his turmoil, John's stress from work mixed with the argument, and he lashed out defensively, saying that Sarah was overreacting and being unreasonable.

As their voices grew louder, the argument escalated further. Past resentments and unrelated issues began creeping into their exchange. They started bringing up old wounds and frustrations, attempting to prove who was more in the wrong.

What had started as a seemingly trivial argument over dirty clothes quickly spiraled into something bigger. Their pent-up frustrations and unexpressed grievances took center stage, overshadowing the initial issue.

Finally, Sarah and John realized how far they had strayed from the original disagreement. The room fell silent as they caught their breaths and took a moment to reflect on the hurtful words that had been exchanged.

With heavy hearts, Sarah and John embraced, realizing their love for each other was stronger than this trivial disagreement and the unnecessary pain they had caused themselves. They vowed to communicate better, to address concerns promptly, and to approach conflict with empathy and understanding.

From that point forward, they committed to actively listening, expressing their needs and emotions honestly, and resolving conflicts before they spiraled into something bigger. They learned that true growth within a relationship comes from recognizing and addressing underlying issues instead of getting caught up in trivial matters.

When an argument shifts away from the original idea, it becomes easy to get overwhelmed and confused by the array of different issues being brought up. This can hinder the progress of finding a resolution as the main problem gets lost in the midst of these unrelated matters. By sticking to one argument, you increase the chances of finding a specific solution to the issue at hand rather than trying to solve multiple problems simultaneously.

Staying committed to addressing one argument also allows both partners to process their emotions and thoughts with patience and understanding. By giving each other the necessary time to fully comprehend and express their feelings, it becomes easier to reach a resolution before moving on to a new topic.

To prevent an argument from going nowhere, it is essential to navigate through the slippery road conditions of the conversation by focusing on one topic at a time. This approach significantly increases the chances of finding a solution that satisfies both partners and contributes to a healthier and more effective communication dynamic.

Communication

Healthy communication is a timeless and essential component of a successful relationship. Active listening is one of the key elements of healthy communication. It involves giving your undivided attention to your partner, making eye contact, and genuinely absorbing what they are saying. By actively listening, you demonstrate respect and show that you value their perspective and opinions.

Furthermore, healthy communication includes responding appropriately to your partner's thoughts and feelings. It is crucial to maintain a conversational tone, ensuring that your responses are respectful, engaged, and open. Non-verbal cues, such as maintaining open body language, can also help convey that you are receptive and attentive to their message.

Using "I" statements is another significant aspect of healthy communication. By expressing your feelings and experiences, rather than assigning blame or making accusatory statements, you create a space for understanding and empathy. This approach encourages your partner to do the same, fostering a safe environment where both individuals feel heard and validated.

Additionally, healthy communication requires the willingness to acknowledge when you are wrong. It takes humility and self-reflection to admit faults and take responsibility for your actions. By being accountable for your mistakes, you demonstrate maturity and a commitment to growth within the relationship.

By incorporating all of these ingredients into your communication, you lay the foundation for a relationship built on love and harmony. Effective communication nurtures understanding, resolves conflict more effectively and cultivates a deeper connection between partners. It is the bedrock upon which a strong and successful relationship can be built, fostering trust, intimacy, and shared growth.

Be Open-Minded

When it comes to resolving conflicts in relationships, one effective technique is to maintain an open-minded attitude throughout disagreements. It is natural to become entrenched in our perspectives and cling to our viewpoints during arguments. However, this narrow-minded approach hinders our ability to be flexible and empathize with our partner's concerns.

In order to foster productive conflict resolution, couples must set aside their egos and approach the situation objectively. This means actively considering both sides of the argument without bias or personal agendas. By adopting this mindset, the door is opened for a reasonable and respectful discussion, where each partner can express their thoughts and feelings without fear of judgment.

Remaining open-minded and objective not only allows for a deeper understanding of our partner's perspective but also increases the likelihood of accepting their viewpoint as valid. This acceptance does not mean agreeing at all times but rather acknowledging and respecting the experiences and feelings that have shaped their viewpoint. By doing so, partners lay the foundation for compromise and finding common ground rather than engaging in a power struggle or escalating conflicts.

When couples consistently practice open-mindedness and objectivity, they are equipping themselves with essential skills for handling the challenges that life inevitably presents. By fostering a climate of understanding and respectful communication, couples are better equipped to navigate disagreements and conflicts, leading to a stronger and more harmonious relationship overall.

Partner's Intentions

It is common to leap to negative conclusions about your partner's behavior in situations where they fall short of your expectations. When your partner forgets to take out the trash, shows up late, or fails to promptly reply to your text, it can be easy to generate a negative interpretation of their actions and respond accordingly.

However, jumping to negative conclusions is not a constructive way to foster a harmonious home environment. Instead, it is essential to take a step back, pause, and reflect on your assumptions. Ask yourself, "What am I assuming here?" and "Is it time to reframe?"

Reframing refers to the ability to consider alternative perspectives and explanations after your mind has defaulted to a negative interpretation. By reframing the situation, you can create space for alternative possibilities and interpretations of your partner's behavior that are positive or neutral rather than negative.

Here's another story to illustrate this for you. Anna and David had been married for many years. They loved each other deeply but often found themselves entangled in confrontations that left them feeling frustrated and disconnected.

One day, after a particularly heated argument over household chores, Anna and David felt exhausted and discouraged. They realized that their confrontations were becoming a pattern, and they wanted to find a way to break free from it.

They decided to seek guidance from a therapist who introduced them to reframing. The therapist explained that reframing involved looking at a situation from a different perspective, with the intention of shifting one's mindset and reactions.

Excited and hopeful, Anna and David decided to apply this idea to their next disagreement. A few days later, they found themselves in a similar situation, arguing over a dispute about finances. But this time, they consciously chose to reframe the situation.

Instead of viewing it as an opportunity to prove who was right, Anna and David took a step back and reminded themselves of their love for each other. They realized that the real issue wasn't about money but their fears and concerns regarding their financial stability and future.

With this newfound perspective, they decided to approach the conversation with empathy and curiosity. They listened to each other's fears and worries, acknowledging that their emotions were valid and deserving of understanding.

They discovered that by reframing the situation and focusing on their shared goals and values, they could collaborate as a team instead of opposing each other. Together, they brainstormed potential solutions and compromises to address their concerns while considering their needs.

As they continued to reframe their confrontations, Anna and David felt a shift in their relationship. Their arguments became less frequent and more constructive. They no longer viewed disagreements as threats to their connection but as opportunities for growth and understanding.

Consider whether there are justifiable reasons for your partner's behavior, such as exhaustion or distraction. Search for positive explanations that put your partner's actions in a more favorable light. Additionally, if you are uncertain about your partner's motives, it is always helpful to seek clarification and ask for their perspective.

By adopting a more positive and open-minded perspective, you can create a healthier and more productive communication dynamic between you and your partner. Avoid jumping to unjustified conclusions and provide space for deeper understanding and empathy to flourish. Ultimately, this will promote a more harmonious and loving relationship.

Chapter Summary

- Effective communication is crucial for positive social interaction and happiness, especially in romantic relationships.

- The communication process involves a sender encoding a message and a receiver decoding it, with feedback and noise affecting the process.

- Personal filters and biases can influence how messages are decoded, making communication more complex.

- According to the Four-Sides model of communication, messages have four facets: factual, self-revelation, relationship, and appeal.

- Individuals may be more attuned to one facet, leading to potential misinterpretations and breakdowns in communication. Understanding and considering all four facets can help improve communication and avoid conflicts.

Chapter 6

Building Lasting Change

"To improve is to change; to be perfect is to change often."
Winston Churchill.

In any relationship, whether it's new or you've been together for years, there are steps you can take to build a healthy and fulfilling connection with your partner. It's important to remember that all relationships go through ups and downs, and they require work, commitment, and a willingness to adapt and grow together.

If you've had past relationship failures or struggled to reignite romance in your current relationship, don't lose hope. Staying connected, finding fulfillment, and experiencing lasting happiness can be achieved through various ways. It all starts with acknowledging that every relationship is unique, and people come together for different reasons. A significant element of a healthy relationship is having a shared objective for what you desire your relationship to be and where you want it to go. This comprehension can only be attained by engaging in profound and truthful conversations with your partner.

One practical exercise to reignite romance in your relationship is to plan a surprise date night. Choose a specific day and time when both of you are free and can dedicate quality time to each other. Pick a theme for your date night that resonates with both your interests or a special memory. It could be a movie night, a picnic in the park, a candlelit dinner at home, or even recreating your first date.

Take the lead and plan all the details for the evening. Arrange for any necessary reservations, buy supplies or ingredients for your chosen activity, and ensure everything is ready. Leave subtle hints or clues for your partner to discover throughout the day leading to the surprise date night. It could be small notes with romantic messages, sending them sweet texts, or leaving a small gift for them to find.

On the day of your surprise date, try to dress up nicely and set a romantic atmosphere. Light candles, play soft music, or decorate your chosen space to create a cozy and intimate ambiance. Once your partner is surprised and you both are on your date, focus on being fully present and enjoying each other's company. Put away distractions, such as phones or work-related thoughts, and enjoy the moment together.

The key to reigniting romance is putting in effort and making your partner feel special. Surprise date nights can help create new memories, strengthen your bond, and remind each other of the love you share.

There are certain characteristics that most healthy relationships have in common, and knowing these principles can help you maintain a meaningful, fulfilling, and exciting connection with your partner, regardless of the challenges you may face. One of these principles is maintaining a meaningful emotional connection with each other. It's not just about being loved, but also feeling loved and emotionally fulfilled. Feeling accepted, valued, and understood by your partner is crucial in creating a strong bond. It's important to avoid getting stuck in a state of peaceful coexistence without truly relating to each other emotionally, as this can create distance in the relationship.

In a healthy relationship, you should not be afraid of respectful disagreement. Every couple handles conflict differently; some prefer calm discussions, while others may express their disagreements more passionately. The key is not to fear conflict but rather to feel safe in expressing your concerns without the fear of backlash. Resolving conflict without resorting to humiliation, degradation, or the desire to always be right is essential.

Maintaining outside relationships and interests is also important in a healthy relationship. It's unrealistic to expect one person to fulfill all your needs. Putting too much pressure on your partner can strain the relationship. It's necessary to sustain your own identity outside of the relationship, maintain connections with friends and family, and nurture your hobbies and interests. Stimulating and enriching your romantic relationship can be achieved with this.

Having open and honest communication is a crucial element of a healthy relationship. Effective communication serves as the basis for any fruitful relationship. When both partners have a clear understanding of what they expect from the relationship and feel at ease expressing their wants and needs, it creates a sense of trust and reinforces the bond. This transparent communication enables growth and facilitates finding ways to tackle challenges and make necessary changes together.

Keep in mind that developing and maintaining a strong relationship is a continuous journey that demands commitment and contribution from both sides. By focusing on maintaining emotional connection, not fearing disagreement, nurturing outside relationships and interests, and communicating openly and honestly, you can create a meaningful and fulfilling partnership with your loved one. This chapter will look at making changes and how to approach it.

Spending Quality Time

When you first fall in love with someone, there is an undeniable connection that comes from looking at and listening to each other. The early stages of a relationship are filled with excitement and new experiences. You likely spent hours talking and finding new things to do together. However, as time goes on and the responsibilities of life start to pile up, finding quality time for each other can become more challenging.

Many couples find that the face-to-face contact they had during the early days of dating is replaced by quick texts, emails, and instant messages. While digital communication has its benefits, it does not have the same positive impact on your brain and nervous system as face-to-face communication. Simply sending a text or a voice message saying "I love you" is nice, but if you rarely make an effort to look at your partner or spend dedicated time together, they may feel that you don't truly understand or appreciate them.

Constantly looking at your partner and giving them undivided attention shows you value and cherish their presence. It demonstrates that you are willing to invest time and energy into nurturing the relationship. Conversely, if you rarely see and engage with your partner, they may feel neglected, unimportant, or misunderstood.

Dedicated time together allows couples to deepen their emotional connection, share experiences, and strengthen their bond. It creates opportunities for meaningful conversations, laughter, physical affection, and creating new memories together. It also helps in reducing anxious attachment in relationships.

To sustain that feeling of falling in love over the long term:

- Make a commitment to spend quality time together on a regular basis.

- Even if you have a busy schedule, take a few minutes each day to put aside your electronic devices and distractions.

- Make a conscious effort to focus on and connect with your partner.

- This could involve having meaningful conversations, sharing your experiences and feelings, or simply enjoying each other's presence.

Additionally, find something that you both enjoy doing together. It could be a shared hobby, taking a dance class, going for a daily walk, or simply sitting down over a cup of coffee in the morning. The activity itself is not as important as the fact that you are doing it together and creating shared experiences. This will strengthen your bond and create lasting memories.

Trying new things together is also important. Doing new activities as a couple can infuse excitement and keep things interesting. It does not have to be extravagant; it can be as simple as trying a new restaurant or going on a day trip to a place you have never been before. The key is to step out of your comfort zone and explore new things together. This will bring a sense of novelty and adventure to your relationship.

Lastly, do not forget to prioritize having fun together. In the early stages of a relationship, couples often have a playful attitude, but as challenges and resentments build up, that playfulness can fade away. Maintaining a sense of humor can help you navigate tough times, reduce stress, and work through issues more easily. Find playful ways to surprise your partner unexpectedly, such as bringing home flowers or booking a table at their favorite restaurant. Playing with pets or spending time with small children can also help you reconnect with your playful side and bring joy into your relationship.

Nurturing your connection and keeping the love alive requires effort, intentional actions, and a commitment to prioritize each other. By consistently looking and listening to each other, spending quality time together, trying new things, and embracing a sense of playfulness, you can keep your relationship strong and thriving.

Do Things Together

One of the most powerful ways to maintain a strong and healthy relationship is to jointly engage in activities that hold meaning and value for both partners outside of the relationship. This could include volunteering for a shared cause, participating in a project together, or engaging in community work that benefits others. By focusing on something that has meaning for both individuals, couples can keep their relationship fresh and interesting while also deepening their bond.

Additionally, engaging in activities to benefit others has been shown to have significant mental health benefits, including reducing stress, anxiety, and depression. Humans have an innate desire to help others, and doing so can bring immense pleasure and fulfillment to individuals and couples alike. Through engaging in community service and other philanthropic activities, couples can not only strengthen their relationship and support a valuable cause but also positively impact the world around them.

Stay Connected

Effective communication is essential for building and maintaining a healthy relationship. When you and your partner have a positive emotional connection and communicate well, you both feel safe, understood, and happy. However, a breakdown in communication can lead to a disconnect, especially during times of change or stress. The good news is that as long as you continue to communicate, you have the ability to work through any challenges you may face.

Expressing your needs to your partner is crucial. It may not always be easy to talk about what you need in the relationship. Many people don't take the time to truly reflect on what is important to them. Furthermore, discussing your needs can make you feel vulnerable, embarrassed, or even ashamed. However, it's important to consider your partner's perspective. Providing comfort and understanding to someone you love should be a pleasure, not a burden.

Even if you have been together for a long time, it's important to remember that your partner is not a mind-reader. While they may have some understanding of your thoughts and needs, it is healthier to express your needs directly to avoid any confusion.

Recognize and pay attention to your partner's nonverbal cues. Much of our communication is conveyed through nonverbal cues such as eye contact, tone of voice, posture, and gestures. These cues often communicate more than words alone. By being attuned to your partner's nonverbal cues, you can better understand their true feelings and respond accordingly. Both you and your partner need to understand each other's nonverbal cues, as people's responses and interpretations may differ. For example, one person may find a hug comforting after a stressful day, while another may prefer to take a walk or have a conversation.

Ensure that your words align with your body language. If you say, "I'm fine," but your clenched teeth and avoided eye contact indicate otherwise, there is a clear mismatch between your verbal and nonverbal communication.

Positive emotional cues play a significant role in fostering a loving and happy relationship. When you show interest in your own and your partner's emotions, you strengthen the connection between you. It is important not to lose sight of emotions, especially during stressful times, as neglecting emotions can strain communication and weaken the relationship.

Being a good listener is just as important as being able to express yourself. By actively listening and making your partner feel valued and understood, you can deepen your connection. Listening goes beyond simply hearing the words spoken. It involves being fully engaged and attentive to your partner's tone of voice, subtle intonations, and the emotions they are trying to convey. Being a good listener does not mean you have to agree with everything your partner says. However, it allows you to find common ground and resolve conflicts more effectively.

During times of stress or emotional overwhelm, it is easy to misinterpret your partner's words or unintentionally send negative nonverbal signals. It can also lead to reactive behaviors that you may later regret. Learning how to manage stress and return to a calm state quickly is crucial not only for avoiding regrets but also for preventing conflicts and misunderstandings. By staying calm, you can also help your partner de-escalate tensions during heated moments.

Physical Intimacy

Touch is an essential aspect of our human experience. Research conducted on infants has highlighted the critical role of regular, affectionate contact in the development of their brains (*CEDARS News*, n.d.). Interestingly, the benefits of touch extend beyond childhood. Affectionate physical contact actually increases the body's production of oxytocin, a hormone that plays a significant role in bonding and attachment.

While sex often holds a central position in committed relationships, it is crucial to recognize that physical intimacy goes beyond sexual encounters. Regular displays of affectionate touches, such as holding hands, hugging, and kissing, are equally important for maintaining a healthy relationship.

However, it is essential to be attentive and considerate of your partner's preferences when it comes to touch. Unwanted or inappropriate touching can cause discomfort and lead the other person to withdraw, which is the opposite effect you aim for. Communication becomes vital in these circumstances, and expressing your needs and intentions clearly to your partner is crucial, just like in other aspects of a healthy relationship.

Even if you and your partner are burdened with hectic work schedules or the demands of raising young children, it is still possible to nurture and prioritize physical intimacy. Setting aside dedicated time for just the two of you can help keep the flame of physical intimacy alive. Whether this takes the form of a regular date night or simply an hour at the end of the day for meaningful conversation or hand-holding, carving out this time demonstrates your commitment to maintaining a deeply connected, intimate relationship.

Give and Take

Understanding and honoring your partner's priorities is a key component of a healthy relationship. Similarly, your partner needs to acknowledge and respect your desires, which must be clearly communicated. Continuously sacrificing your own needs for the sake of others will only breed resentment and anger.

Approaching your partner with an ultimatum mindset, where things must be done your way or else, will hinder the ability to reach a compromise. Such an attitude often stems from unmet needs during childhood or accumulated resentment in the relationship that has reached a breaking point. While it's acceptable to hold strong convictions, it is also crucial to listen to and respect your partner's perspective. Each person should be treated with respect, and their viewpoint should be acknowledged.

Peter and Sally had been together for many years. Despite their love for each other, they often argued over small things and became frustrated with each other's points of view.

One day, Peter came home from work and immediately started complaining about a colleague who had taken credit for his work. Sally listened to his story and sympathized with him but then shared her perspective, saying that maybe the colleague hadn't intended to take credit and it might be worth giving them the benefit of the doubt.

Peter immediately became defensive, believing Sally was taking the colleague's side. He accused her of not trusting him and suggested that she had never supported him in his career. Sally was hurt by this. She had always been his biggest cheerleader and didn't understand why he was attacking her. They went to bed that night feeling angry and distant.

The next day, Peter could see the hurt in Sally's eyes, making him realize he had not been listening to her perspective. He realized she was only trying to help, not to attack or hurt him. He took a deep breath, apologized for his behavior, and asked his wife to explain her point of view again. This time, he listened, respected her perspective, and even saw her point of view. He felt grateful for the fresh perspective and realized his initial reaction had been rash and unfair.

Learning to resolve conflicts respectfully is an important skill in maintaining a strong relationship. Conflict is inevitable, but both individuals must feel heard and understood for the relationship to thrive. The objective should not be to win the argument but rather to preserve and strengthen the connection.

Ensure that fair fighting practices are followed. Keep the focus on the specific issue at hand and maintain respect for the other person. Avoid starting arguments over matters that cannot be changed or resolved.

Instead of directly attacking someone, use "I" statements to express your feelings. For instance, replace "You make me feel bad" with "I feel bad when you do that." Avoid bringing up past arguments or harboring grudges. Instead, focus on finding solutions to the current problem and consider what actions can be taken in the present.

Be willing to forgive. Conflict resolution becomes impossible if you are unwilling or unable to forgive others. Forgiveness allows for healing and moving forward in the relationship.

If emotions become heated, it is important to take a break. Step away for a few minutes to reduce stress and regain composure before saying or doing anything that may be regretted. Always remember that you are arguing with someone you love, and it is essential to handle disagreements with care.

Recognize when it is necessary to let go of an issue. If an agreement cannot be reached, it may be best to agree to disagree. It takes two individuals to prolong an argument, and if it becomes unproductive, disengaging and moving on can be a healthier option.

Ups and Downs

In every relationship, it's important to acknowledge that there will be ups and downs. There will be moments when you and your partner are not on the same page. These differences can stem from various factors, such as individual struggles with personal issues like the loss of a loved one, job loss, or health problems. Additionally, disagreements may arise regarding financial management or parenting styles.

It's crucial to recognize that people cope with stress differently. Misunderstandings that aren't effectively addressed can quickly escalate into frustration and anger.

When dealing with your problems, it's important not to take them out on your partner. Life's stresses can make us short-tempered, and it might seem convenient to vent and even snap at your partner. Fighting in this manner may provide temporary relief, but it gradually poisons the relationship. Instead, seek healthier ways to manage stress, anger, and frustration.

Trying to force a solution can often lead to more problems. Each person uniquely approaches problems and issues. Remember that you are a team, and working together and moving forward can help you overcome challenging times.

Reflecting on the early stages of your relationship can be beneficial. Take the time to revisit the moments that brought you together, identify when you may have started to drift apart, and determine how you can work together to reignite that feeling of falling in love.

Remaining open to change is vital. Change is an inevitable part of life, and it will happen whether you resist or embrace it. Being flexible allows you to adapt to the ongoing changes in any relationship and enables you to grow together during the good and the challenging times.

If you find that your relationship requires external assistance, don't hesitate to seek help together. Sometimes, issues in a relationship can become complex or overwhelming, and it may be beneficial to seek couples therapy or speak with a trusted friend or religious figure who can provide guidance and support. Remember, seeking help is a sign of strength, and it can offer valuable insights and tools for navigating relationship challenges.

Implementing Daily Changes

In life, one often finds happiness in significant events or achievements, such as the joyous occasion of welcoming a new baby into the world, the exhilaration of receiving a well-deserved promotion, or the thrill of winning the lottery and realizing our dreams. These significant milestones undoubtedly bring immense happiness and contentment to our lives.

However, there are also moments when happiness comes from the little things, the seemingly insignificant occurrences that have the power to uplift our spirits. Picture yourself walking to work, engrossed in your thoughts and suddenly you stumble upon a breathtakingly beautiful flower garden. As you stop to take in the vibrant colors and delicate petals, you can't help but feel a profound sense of joy and gratitude. Likewise, imagine meeting up with a friend you haven't seen in ages, and as you embrace each other tightly, a wave of warmth and happiness washes over you.

These small yet meaningful moments of happiness are what we are focusing on here. I believe that incorporating certain adjustments and improvements into your daily routine can have a remarkable impact on your overall well-being, allowing you to experience greater happiness, improved health, and heightened productivity.

By consciously making little changes to your day-to-day activities, you can create opportunities for these happiness boosters to occur more frequently. Whether practicing gratitude, engaging in acts of kindness, taking a few minutes to connect with nature, or simply savoring a delicious meal, these seemingly minor adjustments can make a significant difference in your overall happiness and well-being.

Set Your Daily Ritual

Creating a morning ritual can have a powerful impact on how you start your day. Whether going for a run, meditating, or enjoying a healthy breakfast, engaging in a meaningful activity that energizes you sets a positive and proactive tone for the rest of the day. By establishing a structured start to your day, you can eliminate stress and mental fatigue and enhance your productivity.

A structured start to the day can help set a positive tone and increase productivity. Set a consistent wake-up time that gives you enough hours of sleep for optimal rest. Avoid hitting the snooze button. When your alarm goes off, get out of bed to start your day.

Drink a glass of water or have a cup of warm lemon water to rehydrate your body after a night's sleep. This will also help kickstart your metabolism. Engage in some light stretching or exercise to wake up your body and get the blood flowing. This can be a short yoga routine, a brisk walk, or any form of exercise that suits you.

Practice mindfulness or meditation for a while. You can find a calm and peaceful place, sit in a comfortable position, and concentrate on your breath. Alternatively, you can use a guided meditation app to help you clear your mind and set positive intentions for the day. Take a few minutes to go through your schedule and to-do list. Sort out your tasks in order of priority, and set practical goals for the day. This will help you stay focused and organized.

Remember to allocate time for a breakfast that includes a balance of protein, healthy fats, and carbohydrates. Doing so will help you stay energized throughout the day and maintain your focus. Spend some time engaging in activities that promote personal growth. This could be reading a book, listening to a podcast or audiobook, or learning a new skill or hobby.

Take a moment to reflect on the things you are grateful for in your life. Write down three things you appreciate or say them out loud. This can help shift your mindset towards positivity and create an optimistic outlook for the day. Following this structured routine can set you up for a productive and fulfilling day. Adjust the timings and activities to suit your preferences and commitments, but include activities that promote physical and mental well-being and personal growth.

Surrounding yourself with positive people can significantly impact your happiness. As the saying goes, "You are the average of the five people you spend the most time with." Choose to spend time with individuals who uplift and support you while letting go of toxic relationships. Surrounding yourself with positive influences can create a ripple effect of happiness and positivity in your life.

Regular exercise not only benefits your physical health but also boosts creativity, cognitive abilities, and mood. Exercise releases endorphins, natural chemicals that act as mood boosters and natural anti-depressants. Making time for exercise can be an effective way to energize yourself and improve your overall well-being.

Mastering the art of listening is crucial for effective communication in both personal and professional relationships. Paying attention to others and truly listening not only makes them feel valued but also helps you understand them better and gain new perspectives. Active listening involves being genuinely present, avoiding distractions, and observing non-verbal cues.

Taking a break from social media can have a positive impact on your mental health ("Social Media Breaks: Benefits and Tips to Consider," 2022). With the average person spending a significant amount of time on social media, studies have linked excessive social media usage to higher rates of depression. A social media detox, where you intentionally disconnect from digital platforms for a certain period each day, can reduce stress and mental clutter, allowing you to reconnect with the world around you.

Investing in self-care and taking time to unwind is essential for your overall well-being. Engaging in activities that make you feel good, such as listening to music, learning a new skill, indulging in a relaxing bath, or preparing a delicious meal, can have a significant impact on your mood, mental health, and self-esteem.

Actionable Steps for Immediate Improvement

To start making immediate improvements in your life or work, it's important to first identify and prioritize the areas that need attention. Take some
time to reflect on what specific aspects could benefit from improvement.

Once you have identified these key areas, it's important to set clear and
realistic goals for each one. Ensure that your goals are specific, measurable,
attainable, relevant, and time-bound (Mind Tools, n.d.).

Next, break down each goal into smaller, actionable steps. These steps
should be specific actions you can take to work towards accomplishing
the goal. For example, if your goal is to improve communication skills, a
step could be to enroll in a public speaking course, practice active listening
in your regular conversations, or engage in communication exercises with
your partner, as described in the last chapter.

Start by identifying your long-term and short-term goals for your personal
and professional life. Write them down to keep them at the forefront of
your mind. Prioritize your goals based on their importance and urgency.
This will help you focus on what needs to be done first.

Plan your day or week in advance and allocate specific times to work
on tasks that align with your goals. Use a planner or time management
app to help you stay organized. Avoid distractions such as social media,
personal phone calls, or unnecessary meetings. Use time blocking to focus
on specific tasks and avoid multitasking, often resulting in poorer quality
work.

Take strategic breaks between work times to reset and avoid burnout.
This could be a short yoga routine, reading a chapter from a book, or
simply taking a short walk. Reevaluate your goals and progress regularly

and adjust your plans accordingly. This allows you to stay flexible and adapt to changing circumstances.

Once you have your actionable steps, create a plan or schedule to implement them. Assign specific actions to each day, week, or month, depending on your timeline. This will ensure you have a clear roadmap to follow and help establish a routine.

Taking immediate action is key to making immediate improvements. Don't wait for the perfect moment or for everything to be in place. Start implementing your plan and executing the actionable steps as soon as possible. The sooner you start, the sooner you'll see results.

Don't hesitate to seek support from others. Share your goals and action plan with someone who can hold you accountable and provide guidance or feedback when needed. This could be a mentor, coach, colleague, or friend. Having someone to support and encourage you can help keep you motivated and focused.

Practice self-reflection and continuous improvement. Take time to reflect on your actions, achievements, and areas that still need improvement. Learn from your experiences, adjust your approach if necessary, and keep striving for growth and improvement. This ongoing self-reflection will help you maintain a mindset of continuous learning and development.

Seeking Support

Seeking support is a valuable step towards bringing about lasting change. Here are some actionable steps to help you find the support you need:

- **Identify your support network:** Make a list of individuals or groups who could potentially offer the support you need. This could include friends, family members, mentors, colleagues, or professionals in the field you are looking to improve.

- **Share your goals and aspirations:** Reach out to the people in your support network and explain your goals and aspirations. Be open and honest about what you are trying to achieve and the kind of support you are seeking. This will help them understand how they can best support you.

- **Seek guidance from mentors or coaches:** If you have specific areas of improvement in mind, consider finding a mentor or coach who specializes in those areas. They can provide targeted guidance, share expertise, and offer personalized strategies for lasting change.

- **Join communities or groups with similar interests:** Look for communities or groups focused on the area you want to improve. This could be an online community, a local meetup, or a professional organization. Engaging with like-minded individuals can provide support, encouragement, and new perspectives.

- **Attend workshops or training programs:** Seek out workshops or training programs that align with your goals for lasting change. These can be valuable opportunities to learn new skills, gain insights, and connect with others who share similar aspirations. Take advantage of these resources to strengthen your support network and deepen your understanding.

- **Build accountability partnerships:** Find an accountability partner or form a small group of individuals striving for lasting change. Regularly meet or check in with each other to review progress, share challenges, and provide support and encouragement.

- **Be open to feedback and advice:** When seeking support, be open to receiving feedback and advice from others. Sometimes, outside perspectives can provide valuable insights and help you see blind spots or areas for improvement you may have overlooked.

Seeking support is not a sign of weakness but rather a sign of strength and an acknowledgment that you are committed to making lasting changes. By reaching out, leveraging your support network, and being open to guidance, you can enhance your chances of bringing about the change you desire and then recovering from anxious attachment.

The Role of Friends and Family in the Recovery Process

Friends and family play a crucial role in the recovery process of an individual facing anxious attachment or undergoing a personal struggle. Here are some ways in which friends and family can support someone in their recovery:

- **Emotional support:** Friends and family provide emotional support by offering empathy, understanding, and compassion. They can be a safe space for the individual to express their feelings, frustrations, and fears. By actively listening and validating their emotions, friends and family contribute to the person's overall well-being, self-esteem, and motivation to recover.

- **Encouragement and motivation:** Friends and family can serve as a source of encouragement and motivation throughout the recovery process. They can remind the person of their progress, praise their achievements, and provide positive reinforcement. This support can help bolster the individual's confidence and belief in their ability to overcome challenges.

- **Practical assistance:** Friends and family can offer practical assistance by helping with daily tasks or responsibilities that the person may struggle with during recovery. This can include cooking meals, running errands, attending appointments together, or providing transportation. By alleviating some practical burdens, they enable the person to focus on their recovery.

- **Accountability and structure:** Friends and family can play a role in keeping the individual accountable to their recovery goals. They can check in regularly, ask about progress, and gently remind them of their commitments. By providing structure and holding the person accountable, friends and family contribute to maintaining a sense of discipline and commitment.

- **Providing a supportive environment:** Creating a supportive and nurturing environment is crucial for a successful recovery process. Friends and family can help establish boundaries, set a positive atmosphere, and support the person's healthy choices. They may also remove triggers or unhealthy influences from the person's surroundings, making it easier for them to stay on track.

- **Education and research:** Friends and family can educate themselves about the specific challenges the person is facing. By learning about the condition, treatment options, and recovery strategies, they can better understand the person's experiences and provide more informed support. This knowledge allows them to communicate effectively and assist in finding appropriate resources.

- **Seeking professional help together:** Friends and family can actively participate in the recovery process by attending therapy sessions or support groups together with the person. This shows solidarity and signals their commitment to supporting the individual's recovery. In some cases, family therapy or counseling can help address underlying family dynamics or communication patterns that may impact the person's recovery.

It's important to note that supportive friends and family members should also take care of their well-being to avoid burnout. Seeking support from other sources, such as support groups or therapy, can be beneficial for them, too.

Overall, friends and family contribute significantly to a person's recovery process by providing emotional support, encouragement, practical assistance, accountability, and a nurturing environment. Their involvement can greatly enhance the individual's chances of successfully overcoming challenges and achieving long-term recovery.

Celebrating Progress

Recognizing and celebrating progress is a fundamental aspect of the journey towards healing from anxious attachment. In the pursuit of a more secure attachment style, it becomes essential to applaud the incremental steps taken, both big and small. These celebratory moments play a pivotal role in boosting confidence and sustaining the motivation required to continue cultivating a healthier attachment style.

Breaking down the recovery journey into manageable milestones provides a clear roadmap for personal growth. Each milestone achieved signifies a triumph over anxious attachment patterns, marking a positive shift towards greater emotional security. By acknowledging these steps, individuals can reinforce their commitment to change and build a foundation for a more fulfilling connection with others.

To enhance the celebratory aspect of progress, incorporating a reward system can be both motivating and enjoyable. Establishing a range of rewards, from simple treats like indulging in a favorite dessert or treating yourself to a movie to more substantial rewards such as a weekend getaway or a coveted purchase, creates a tangible connection between achievement and positive reinforcement.

The choice of rewards should align with personal preferences and aspirations, making each milestone a personalized and meaningful victory. This not only adds an element of excitement to the journey but also serves as a reminder of the progress made and the resilience demonstrated in overcoming anxious attachment tendencies.

Crucially, amidst the celebration of achievements, it is paramount to maintain a compassionate and gentle approach towards oneself. Recognizing that the journey towards a more secure attachment style is a process of growth and self-discovery allows for a kinder perspective. Embracing both the big and small victories fosters a nurturing environment for personal transformation.

In summary, the practice of celebrating progress in the journey towards healing from anxious attachment contributes significantly to building resilience and fortifying the commitment to change. By breaking the recovery process into small, achievable milestones and attaching meaningful rewards to these accomplishments, individuals can create a positive feedback loop that fuels motivation and reinforces the pursuit of a healthier attachment style. Remembering to be gentle with oneself throughout this journey ensures that each step forward is not only acknowledged but cherished as a significant victory on the path to emotional well-being.

Chapter Summary

- Building a healthy relationship takes work, commitment, and a willingness to adapt and change with your partner, regardless of the length of the relationship or past relationship failures.

- Communication with your partner regarding shared goals and understanding the basic principles of healthy relationships are essential to keep the relationship meaningful, fulfilling, and exciting.

- Successful couples maintain a meaningful emotional connection with each other and are unafraid of respectful disagreement.

- Couples keep outside relationships and interests alive as no single person can meet all their needs.

- Open and honest communication is key in any successful relationship as it increases trust and strengthens the bond between two people.

Conclusion

"Anxious attachment stems from a deep sense of inner instability where old wounds make people anticipate that they will be abandoned again and again."

Jessica Baum.

In conclusion, *Anxious Attachment Recovery* is a comprehensive guidebook that provides valuable insights and practical strategies for individuals seeking to heal from anxious attachment patterns and build healthier, more secure relationships. The book's main ideas revolve around understanding the origins and impacts of anxious attachment, identifying and challenging anxious thoughts and behaviors, and developing new patterns of secure attachment.

I introduced the concept of attachment theory, explaining how early childhood experiences shape our attachment styles. I emphasized that anxious attachment often stems from inconsistent or unpredictable caregiving during childhood, leading to a deep-seated fear of abandonment and a constant need for reassurance and validation in relationships.

One of the key takeaways is the importance of recognizing and understanding one's attachment style. By becoming aware of the patterns and triggers associated with anxious attachment, individuals can begin to unravel the root causes of their anxiety. I also provided various self-assessment exercises and reflective prompts to help you gain insight into your attachment style and how it manifests in your relationships.

I also highlighted the significance of self-compassion and self-care in the recovery process. Anxious individuals often tend to blame themselves for their attachment anxieties, which only reinforces the cycle of insecurity. I also encourage you to practice self-compassion and develop healthy self-care routines that prioritize your emotional well-being.

Another central theme was the need for clear and effective communication. Anxious individuals often struggle with expressing their needs and boundaries for fear of pushing their partners away. I provided practical tips and scripts for initiating difficult conversations, setting boundaries, and expressing needs in a non-accusatory and assertive manner.

Furthermore, I delved into the importance of establishing trust and security in relationships. I explored strategies and techniques for building trust with a partner and creating a safe emotional space where both partners feel valued and understood. I emphasized the importance of consistent and reliable behavior and guided how to foster open and honest communication.

I also offered a range of techniques to help individuals manage their anxious thoughts and reduce their emotional reactivity. By learning to observe and challenge your anxious thoughts, you can gain a sense of control over your emotions and develop more constructive responses in your relationships.

I also spoke about the concept of boundaries and emphasized their role in cultivating healthier relationships. I stressed the importance of setting clear boundaries and assertively communicating them to one's partner. Additionally, I explored the significance of boundaries in managing expectations, promoting self-worth, and maintaining individual autonomy within the relationship.

An important aspect of *Anxious Attachment Recovery* is developing new patterns of secure attachment. It guides how to cultivate and nurture secure attachment styles, which involve consistently meeting one's own emotional needs and fostering a sense of security and trust within oneself. It offered strategies for building self-confidence, developing emotional resilience, and embracing vulnerability in relationships.

Overall, *Anxious Attachment Recovery* offered a wealth of information and practical tools for individuals seeking to heal from anxious attachment patterns. By gaining insight into their attachment style, practicing self-compassion, improving communication skills, and cultivating secure attachment within themselves, readers can work towards building healthier and more fulfilling relationships. Recovery is a gradual and ongoing process and encourages individuals to be patient and persistent in their journey toward healing and growth.

Now that you have gained valuable insights and practical strategies, it's time to take action and apply what you've learned to your own life and relationships. Here are a few tips to help you get started:

- **Reflect on your attachment style:** Take some time to reflect on your attachment style and how it manifests in your relationships. Consider the patterns and triggers that contribute to your anxious attachment. This self-awareness is the first step towards healing and growth.

- **Practice self-compassion and self-care:** Recognize that anxious attachment is not your fault. Be gentle with yourself and practice self-compassion. Implement self-care routines that prioritize your emotional well-being. Prioritizing your own needs will help you build a stronger sense of self and create a more secure foundation for your relationships.

- **Communicate effectively:** Work on improving your communication skills by being clear and assertive about your needs and boundaries. Use the techniques and scripts provided in the book to initiate difficult conversations and express yourself in a constructive and non-accusatory manner. Effective communication is essential for building trust and understanding in your relationships.

- **Challenge anxious thoughts:** Practice mindfulness and cognitive restructuring exercises to observe and challenge your anxious thoughts. By questioning the validity of these thoughts and replacing them with more realistic and positive ones, you can reduce your emotional reactivity and gain a sense of control over your emotions.

- **Set clear boundaries:** Take the time to identify your boundaries and communicate them to your partner. Boundaries are crucial for maintaining a healthy balance in a relationship and establishing a sense of safety and respect. Be assertive in setting and enforcing your boundaries, ensuring that your needs are met and that you maintain your autonomy.

- **Build secure attachment within yourself:** Focus on nurturing a sense of security and trust within yourself. Practice self-reliance, build self-confidence, and cultivate emotional resilience. Embrace vulnerability in your relationships, as vulnerability is a key ingredient in deepening emotional connections and building secure attachment bonds.

Remember, applying the knowledge and strategies outlined in this book will require patience, persistence, and a commitment to personal growth.

Be prepared for setbacks and obstacles along the way, but stay focused on your intention to heal and build healthier relationships.

By taking action and applying what you've learned, you have the opportunity to break free from anxious attachment patterns and create a more secure and fulfilling future for yourself and your relationships. Begin your journey of transformation today and experience the positive impact it can have on your life.

With knowledge and commitment, I am pretty sure you will achieve your goals!

Note From The Author

Hi!

First and foremost, I'd like to thank you for reading this book and for coming this far.

I really hope you feel confident and prepared to overcome your challenges. I am sure you will do it!

Second, if you enjoyed reading this book, I humbly ask that you **consider writing an honest review** about your experience. Your act of kindness will help me so much. Thank you in advance!

Just scan the QR code below:

Finally, don't forget to grab your free copy of "**Communication Skills for Lasting Love**," also offered at the beginning of this book. This guide will provide deeper insights into ways to improve communication in your relationship and help you overcome your anxious attachment.

Sincerely,

Amy Harper

Glossary

- **Attachment Theory:** A psychological framework that explains how early childhood experiences shape our attachment styles and influence our adult relationships.

- **Anxious Attachment:** A style of attachment characterized by a deep-seated fear of abandonment, a constant need for reassurance and validation, and a tendency to be overly sensitive to relationship cues.

- **Secure Attachment:** A style of attachment characterized by trust, emotional security, and a healthy balance of independence and interdependence in relationships.

- **Reflective Prompts:** Questions or statements designed to encourage self-reflection and deeper exploration of one's thoughts, emotions, and behaviors.

- **Blame:** The act of attributing fault or responsibility to oneself or others. Anxious individuals often engage in self-blame, holding themselves accountable for their attachment anxieties.

- **Self-Compassion:** The practice of extending kindness, understanding, and forgiveness to oneself when facing difficulties or setbacks.

- **Emotional Reactivity:** The tendency to have intense emotional responses to certain triggers or situations, often resulting in impulsive or heightened reactions.

- **Mindfulness:** The practice of cultivating present-moment awareness and non-judgmental acceptance of one's thoughts, feelings, and sensations.

- **Cognitive Restructuring:** A technique that involves identifying and challenging negative or irrational thought patterns and replacing them with more realistic and positive ones.

- **Grounding Techniques:** Strategies that help individuals connect with the present moment, such as deep breathing, sensory awareness, or focusing on physical sensations.

- **Boundaries:** The limits and guidelines one sets for themselves and their relationships to establish healthy emotional and physical boundaries.

- **Effective Communication:** Clear and open communication that fosters understanding, empathy, and connection in relationships.

- **Self-Reliance:** The ability to meet one's emotional needs and have a sense of independence and self-sufficiency.

- **Emotional Resilience:** The ability to adapt, cope with, and recover from emotional challenges and stressful situations.

- **Vulnerability:** The willingness to be open, sincere, and exposed in relationships, allowing for deeper emotional connections and trust.

- **Trust:** The process of developing trust and creating a safe emotional space in relationships through consistent and reliable behavior.

References

Amir Levine Quotes (Author of Attached). (n.d.). www.goodreads.com. Retrieved December 9, 2023, from https://www.goodreads.com/author/quotes/4417525.Amir_Levine

Anxious Attachment Quotes (6 quotes). (n.d.). www.goodreads.com. Retrieved December 1, 2023, from https://www.goodreads.com/quotes/tag/anxious-attachment#:~:text=Don

Anxious Attachment Quotes (6 quotes). (n.d.-b). www.goodreads.com. Retrieved December 8, 2023, from https://www.goodreads.com/quotes/tag/anxious-attachment#:~:text=%E2%80%9CI%20think%20about

Anxiously Attached Quotes by Jessica Baum. (n.d.). www.goodreads.com. Retrieved November 28, 2023, from https://www.goodreads.com/work/quotes/94317849-anxiously-attached-becoming-more-secure-in-life-and-love#:~:text=If%20you%20are%20in%20love

Attachment disorder in adults: Symptoms, causes, and more. (2020, October 30). www.medicalnewstoday.com. https://www.medicalnewstoday.com/articles/attachment-disorder-in-adults#relationships

Brennan, D. (2021, April 8). What is anxious attachment? WebMD. https://www.webmd.com/mental-health/what-is-anxious-attachment

Cherry, K. (2022, May 26). The different types of attachment styles. Verywell Mind. https://www.verywellmind.com/attachment-styles-2795344

Do your early experiences affect your adult relationships? (2016, March 12). Psych Central. https://psychcentral.com/blog/how-childhood-trauma-affects -adult-relationships#:~:text=Trust%20challenges

Domendos. (2021, May 28). 4 Sides model of communication. Projectman agement.guide. https://projectmanagement.guide/4-sides-model-of-commu nication/

Erozkan, A. (2016). The link between types of attachment and childhood trauma. Universal Journal of Educational Research, 4(5), 1071–1079. ht tps://doi.org/10.13189/ujer.2016.040517

Freed, M. (2023, June 12). 10 Ways to improve communication in your marriage and strengthen your relationship. Freed Marcroft LLC. https://freedmarcroft.com/10-ways-to-improve-communication-in-yo ur-marriage-and-strengthen-your-relationship/

Gorlick, A. (2016, April 16). Media multitaskers pay mental price, Stanford study shows. Stanford News; Stanford University. https://news.stanford.ed u/2009/08/24/multitask-research-study-082409/

Lebow, H. I. (2022, June 22). Anxious attachment style: What it looks like in adult relationships. Psych Central. https://psychcentral.com/health/anxi ous-attachment-style-signs

Madrid, E. (2012). Facebook.com. https://www.facebook.com/verywell

Mark Manson. (2021, January 13). Attachment Theory. Mark Manson. https://markmanson.net/attachment-styles

Mikulincer, M., & Shaver, P. R. (2009). An attachment and behavioral systems perspective on social support. Journal of Social and Personal Rela- tionships, 26(1), 7–19. https://doi.org/10.1177/0265407509105518

*Mind Tools. (n.d.). SMART Goals. Mind Tools. https://www.mindtools.co
m/a4wo118/smart-goals*

*Moore, C. (2019, June 2). How to practice self-compassion: 8 Techniques and
tips. Positive Psychology. https://positivepsychology.com/how-to-practice-self
-compassion/*

*National Collaborating Centre for Mental Health (UK). (2015). Introduc-
tion to children's attachment. Nih.gov; National Institute for Health and
Care Excellence (UK). https://www.ncbi.nlm.nih.gov/books/NBK356196/*

*News from CEDARS. (n.d.). Cedarskids.org. Retrieved December 26, 2023,
f   r   o   m
https://cedarskids.org/news/news.html/article/2021/08/11/hold-me-close-ph
ysical-touch-and-brain-development#:~:text=In%20this%20way%2C%20n
urturing%20physical*

*Past Experiences Quotes (13 quotes). (n.d.). www.goodreads.com. Retrieved
December   8,   2023,   from
https://www.goodreads.com/quotes/tag/past-experiences#:~:text=%E2%80%
9CLearn%20from%20past%20experiences%20but%20accept%20them%20
all%20as%20perfect%20while%20staying%20in%20the%20present.%20Let
%20go%20of%20everything%20that%20doesn%27t%20serve%20you.%E2%
80%9D*

*Reflective   Listening | UNSW   Teaching   Staff   Gateway.   (n
.d.).   www.teaching.unsw.edu.au.   Retrieved   December   26,   2023,
from https://www.teaching.unsw.edu.au/group-work-reflective-listening#:
~:text=Reflective%20listening%20appears%20deceptively%20easy*

*Riggs, S. A. (2010). Childhood emotional abuse and the attachment system
across the life cycle: What theory and research tell us. Journal of Aggression,*

Maltreatment & Trauma, 19(1), 5–51. https://doi.org/10.1080/1092677 0903475968

Rising above the Imposter Syndrome trap on women & minorities. (n.d.). Hospitalityinsights.ehl.edu. https://hospitalityinsights.ehl.edu/imposter-syn drome-women-minorities

Ross, E. J., Graham, D. L., Money, K. M., & Stanwood, G. D. (2015). Developmental consequences of fetal exposure to drugs: What we know and what we still must learn. Neuropsychopharmacology, 40(1), 61–87. https:/ /doi.org/10.1038/npp.2014.147

Schröder, M., Lüdtke, J., Fux, E., Izat, Y., Bolten, M., Gloger-Tippelt, G., Suess, G. J., & Schmid, M. (2019). Attachment disorder and attachment theory–Two sides of one medal or two different coins? Comprehensive Psychiatry, 95(95), 152139. https://doi.org/10.1016/j.comppsych.2019.152139

7 Telltale signs of an anxiously attached partner | Psychology Today. (n.d.). www.psychologytoday.com. Retrieved December 26, 2023, from https://www.psychologytoday.com/intl/blog/narcissism-demystified/202306/ 7-telltale-signs-of-an-anxiously-attached-partner#:~:text=6.%20Anxiously %20attached%20partners%20feel%20one%2Ddown%20in%20a%20relatio nship.

Social media breaks: Benefits and tips to consider. (2022, May 12). Www.medicalnewstoday.com . https://www.medicalnewstoday.com/articles/social-media-breaks#:~:text =Eases%20anxiety&text=Social%20media%20use%20can%20cause

35 Quotes about communication for inspiring team collaboration | Vibe. (n.d.). Vibe.us. https://vibe.us/blog/35-quotes-about-communication/#:~:tex t=%E2%80%9CCommunication%20is%20the%20solvent%20of

Winston Churchill Quotes. (n.d.). BrainyQuote. https://www.brainyquote. com/quotes/winston_churchill_138235

Work less and do more by applying the Pareto Principle to your task list. (2012, June 1). Lifehacker. https://lifehacker.com/work-less-and-do-more-b y-applying-the-pareto-principle-5914877